Why Catholics Cannot Be Masons

> *"Whosoever revolteth, and continueth not in the doctrine of Christ, hath not God. . . . If any man come to you, and bring not this doctrine, receive him not into the house nor say to him, 'God speed you.' For he that saith unto him, 'God speed you,' communicateth with his wicked works."*
>
> —2 John 1:9-11

Why Catholics Cannot Be Masons

By

John Salza

"Bear not the yoke with unbelievers. For what participation hath justice with injustice? Or what fellowship hath light with darkness? And what concord hath Christ with Belial? Or what part hath the faithful with the unbeliever? And what agreement hath the temple of God with idols? For you are the temple of the living God. . . . Wherefore, Go out from among them, and be ye separate, saith the Lord, and touch not the unclean thing." —2 Corinthians 6:14-17

TAN Books
Charlotte, North Carolina

Nihil Obstat: Charles McNamee, J.C.L.
                    Censor Librorum

Imprimatur: ✠ Thomas G. Doran, D.D., J.C.D.
                    Bishop of Rockford
                    July 21, 2008

Grateful acknowledgment to Our Sunday Visitor Press for permission to use material from the glossary of *Masonry Unmasked,* by John Salza, OSV, 2006.

ISBN 978-0-89555-881-7

Cover design by Milo Persic. The upper panel shows the Chi Rho (pronounced Kee-Roe and formed from the X and P of the Greek alphabet), a symbol of Christ, along with the Alpha and Omega, the first and last letters of the Greek alphabet, which together represent God. In *Apocalypse* 1:8 these letters are used to designate the Eternal Father and in *Apocalypse* 21:6 and 22:13 God the Son as eternal, self-existent, infinite being itself. "I am Alpha and Omega, the beginning and the end, saith the Lord God. . . ." (*Apoc.* 1:8). (Attwater, *Catholic Dictionary,* p. 16). The lower panel features the Masonic square and compass and letter G; the G stands for God and Geometry.

Printed and bound in the United States of America.

TAN Books
Charlotte, North Carolina
www.TANBooks.com
2015

To the Blessed Virgin Mary,
Who, as "Our Lady of Good Success"
at Quito, Ecuador,
warned of the evil of Masonry,
And who will conquer all heresies through the
Triumph of her Immaculate Heart.

About the Author

An author, lawyer and noted Catholic apologist, John Salza is a former 32nd Degree Scottish Rite Freemason and Shriner. He was a member of two Masonic Lodges in Milwaukee, serving as Junior Deacon, Senior Deacon and Junior Warden. The Grand Lodge of Wisconsin awarded him the distinguished Proficiency Card in recognition of his expertise in Masonic ritual. This credential authorized him to instruct other Masons in how to perform the rituals of Freemasonry. In addition to teaching Masonic ritual, John Salza proposed many changes to Wisconsin's Masonic ritual, which were adopted by the Masonic Grand Lodge of Wisconsin. He also played major roles in performing the rituals of Scottish Rite Freemasonry and the Shriners.

After investigating the Catholic Church's teachings on Freemasonry, Salza renounced his Masonic membership in 1999. In thanksgiving to God for the grace he had received, he has devoted himself to Catholic apologetics. He created the popular website www.ScriptureCatholic.com and is the author of the following books published by Our Sunday Visitor: *Masonry Unmasked: An Insider Reveals the Secrets of the Lodge; The Biblical Basis for the Catholic Faith; The Biblical Basis for the Papacy; The Biblical Basis for the Eucharist; The Biblical Basis for Tradition,* and *The Biblical Basis for Purgatory.* John Salza is a frequent guest and host on Catholic radio and has his own daily feature on Relevant Radio: "Relevant Answers." Mr. Salza has also appeared on Eternal Word Television Network (EWTN), and he has a daily apologetics program on EWTN Radio called "Catholic Q&A."

Contents

1. A Harmless Fraternal Organization?   1
2. The History and Purpose of Freemasonry   5
3. An Introduction to the Errors of Freemasonry   9
4. Preparation for the First Degree   18
5. Spiritual Darkness   20
6. Freemasonry's Worship of "Deity"   24
7. Who Is the God of Freemasonry?   28
8. Freemasonry's Profession of Faith in the Deity   31
9. Freemasonry's Oaths   34
10. Freemasonry's View of the Holy Bible   38
11. Freemasonry's Salvation by Works   41
12. Freemasonry's Doctrine of Resurrection
    of the Body   45
13. The Clear, Consistent Teaching of the Church   50
14. Conclusion   58
    Further Reading   59
Appendix A: Papal Condemnations of Freemasonry   60
Appendix B: "No Salvation Outside the Church"   62
Appendix C: Recent Restatement of the Church's
            Condemnation   64
Appendix D: Resigning from Freemasonry   66
Notes   70
Glossary of Terms   79

Why Catholics Cannot Be Masons

"He that believeth and is baptized, shall be saved: but he that believeth not shall be condemned."

—Mark 16:16

—1—
A Harmless Fraternal Organization?

"Remember that Christianity and Masonry are essentially irreconcilable, such that to join one is to divorce the other." —Pope Leo XIII[1]

Many people believe that Masonry—also called Freemasonry—is a harmless fraternal organization devoted to making good men better and to helping society at large. They see little difference between Masonry and fraternities such as the Knights of Columbus. Like the Knights of Columbus, Masons conduct fundraising activities, donate money to charities and hold social events for their members and families. Masons are often upstanding citizens who profess a love for God and neighbor. Many prominent men of society have also been Masons. In light of these characteristics, many people—including some Catholic priests—do not understand the reason for the Catholic Church's opposition to Freemasonry. Why is that?

Primarily it is because the general public has no idea what Freemasonry teaches inside its lodge rooms about God and salvation. When a man becomes a Mason, he is required to swear oaths of secrecy, promising never to reveal the teachings of the Lodge. The Mason swears these oaths at an altar, on the Bible (if he is Christian), and under symbolic penalties of mutilation and death. He is repeatedly warned that if he ever revealed the teachings of the Order to non-Masons (whom Masonry terms "profanes"), he would be worthy of the death penalty and "the contempt and detestation of all good Masons."[2]

Because most Masons take these warnings seriously, they do not reveal Freemasonry's secret religious teachings to non-Masons. Instead, when discussing their organization with "profanes," Masons focus on the positive aspects of Masonry, such as its social or charitable activities. They concentrate on how much good Masonry does and not on what Masonry teaches. Thus, the public's understanding of Freemasonry comes almost exclusively from what it sees and hears *from Masons*. This understanding invariably excludes any knowledge of Masonry's explicit teachings about its deistic understanding of God, its belief in salvation by works, and its most sublime religious doctrine—the resurrection of the body.

The Catholic Church, of course, knows better. As the spotless Bride of Christ who is guided by the Holy Ghost, she knows when error threatens the souls of her members. She knows when heretical teaching seeks to undermine Catholic truth. This is why no fewer than 12 Popes have individually issued two dozen condemnations of Freemasonry since 1738 on the grounds that Masonry's teachings are incompatible with the Catholic Faith. (See Appendix A for a list of these pronouncements.) The Church has declared that any Catholic who joins Freemasonry puts himself in a state of grave (that is, mortal) sin and cannot receive the Eucharist.

Many "Catholic" Masons in the United States are

quick to dismiss the perennial teachings of the Popes as not relevant to their personal situations. They pretend that the Church's repeated condemnations apply only to European Masonry, but not to their American lodges or rituals. Some even contend that the Popes' condemnations were politically motivated. In other words, they convince themselves that the Vicars of Christ were ignorant and made rash judgments against Masonry. This is a most serious error.

The Church is clear that her condemnations apply to Freemasonry wherever it exists, both in America and abroad.[3] Further, the Church has specifically dismissed any distinctions among the various versions and degrees of Freemasonry because they all inculcate the same religious errors.[4] As this book demonstrates, the Popes' condemnations of Freemasonry are based *on the unchanging truths of Catholic faith and morals.* This means they apply to all Catholics. These condemnations are especially relevant today as we struggle under what Cardinal Joseph Ratzinger, the day before he was elected Pope, called a "dictatorship of relativism."

When evaluating the weight of these condemnations, Catholics must remember that the Pope is the Vicar of Christ and the successor of St. Peter. Through the power of the keys, Jesus Christ confirms in Heaven what Peter and his successors bind or loose on earth. (See *Matthew* 16:18-19).[5] This means that Christ protects from error the Pope's official teachings on faith

---

Note: In this book we are using quotation marks around the word "Catholic" in the term "Catholic Mason" because if a Catholic has accepted the teachings of Masonry, knowing their contradiction to Catholic teaching yet embracing them anyway, he is in fact no longer a Catholic.

and morals, and Catholics must accept the truth of these teachings in order to have a genuine hope of eternal life. To disregard the Popes' consistent teachings and their authority over Catholics is to disregard Christ Himself and imperil one's own salvation. As Pope Boniface VIII affirmed: "We declare, say, define and pronounce that it is absolutely necessary for the salvation of every human creature to be subject to the Roman Pontiff."[6]

This book explains the doctrinal basis for the Popes' repeated condemnations of Freemasonry. It highlights the reasons why the Church's prohibitions are based on Catholic faith and morals. It helps "tear away the mask from Freemasonry . . . to let it be seen as it really is."[7] It explains *Why Catholics Cannot Be Masons*.

—2—

The History and Purpose of Freemasonry

From Operative to Speculative Freemasonry

Before we address the theology of Freemasonry, let us briefly review some background on the organization. Most Masons trace the origins of Freemasonry back to the ancient stonemasons' guilds that built the great cathedrals of Europe. Because these highly skilled craftsmen were independent contractors and not indentured servants, they were known as "free masons."

According to Masonic tradition, free masons began to organize themselves into lodges, where they would meet and share trade secrets. Over time, the free masons began admitting philosophers, merchants and other non-masons into their lodges. These were called "accepted" masons. Eventually, the "Free and Accepted Masons" changed from an organization of "operative" masons—those who built physical structures, to "speculative" masons—those who build the "spiritual temple," a Masonic metaphor for the soul. The *Masonic Bible,* a popular teaching tool used by Freemasons, says that building the "spiritual edifice" of the Mason is the "supreme end of Freemasonry."[1] The terms "Masonry" and "Freemasonry" came to be used interchangeably, and they are used interchangeably today.

The date that marked the formal transition from operative to speculative Freemasonry occurred on June 24, 1717 during the heart of the Enlightenment period. On this date, four Masonic lodges in London founded the Grand Lodge of England. Masons generally view this event as the birth of modern Freemasonry. The Grand Lodge of England developed the blueprint for the Masonic rituals and ceremonies that are used today in the United States and throughout the world.

The Goal of Freemasonry Is to Lead Its Members to Heaven

By building the spiritual temple of the individual Mason, Freemasonry believes it leads its members to Heaven. The *Masonic Bible* says, "By the practice of Freemasonry, its members may advance their spirituality, and mount by the theological ladder from the Lodge on earth to the Lodge in heaven."[2] Albert Mackey, a prominent Masonic author, also says that Freemasonry provides Masons "with the means of advancing from earth to heaven, from death to life—from the mortal to immortality."[3]

Henry Wilson Coil, another popular Masonic author, says that many Masons get to Heaven with "no other guarantee of a safe landing than their belief in the religion of Freemasonry."[4] Freemasonry advances the spirituality of its members through its secret moral and doctrinal teachings which are symbolized by the working tools of the old operative Masons. These include the Square, Compass, Level, Plumb and Trowel. The universal symbol of Freemasonry is the Square and Compass (which sometimes includes the letter G in the middle).

The Structure of Freemasonry

The basic organizational unit of Freemasonry is the Blue (or Symbolic) Lodge. Each Blue Lodge comes under the authority of the Grand Lodge. In the United States, there are fifty-one Grand Lodges (one for each state and the District of Columbia). The chief officer of the Blue Lodge is called the "Worshipful Master." In the Blue Lodge, the candidate studies for and receives the three Masonic degrees called "Entered Apprentice," "Fellowcraft" and "Master Mason."

A Master Mason in good standing may join either the Scottish Rite or the York Rite of Freemasonry. These are optional Masonic organizations that elaborate on the religious teachings of the Blue Lodge. In the United States, a 32nd degree Scottish Rite or York Rite Mason may join the "Ancient Arabic Order, Nobles of the Mystic Shrine"—known as the "Shriners."[5] The Shriners are known for their red hats, circuses and parades and sponsorship of hospitals.[6] While not all Masons are Shriners, all Shriners are Masons. According to Freemasonry's own estimates, there are approximately 6 million Masons worldwide, with 4 million of them in the United States.

While each Grand Lodge is sovereign and independent, the Masonic ritual that the Grand Lodges practice is essentially the same. The ritual is the same because Freemasonry is built upon certain unalterable principles called "Landmarks." Landmarks are the universal teachings of Freemasonry handed down through Masonic ritual and oral tradition. Albert Mackey says that the "doctrine of Freemasonry is everywhere the same. It is the Body which is unchangeable—remaining always and everywhere the same."[7] Freemasonry's Landmarks include its belief in God as the Great Architect of the Universe, covenant oaths, the immortality of the soul and the resurrection of the body.

—3—

An Introduction to the Errors of Freemasonry

Freemasonry Denies the Uniqueness of Jesus Christ and His Church

While Freemasonry claims that it can build the spiritual temple of its members, it denies any need for Jesus Christ or the Catholic Church. Masonry ignores the teachings of Jesus Christ, who declared, "I am the way and the truth and the life. No man comes to the Father, but by me." (*John* 14:6). Instead, Masonry believes that any Mason, no matter what religion he professes, will share eternal beatitude with God. Thus, Freemasonry denies the infallible dogma repeatedly proclaimed by Popes and Councils throughout the centuries: "Outside the Church there is no salvation." (See Appendix B for a list of these pronouncements.)

Restated positively, this dogma means that all salvation comes from Jesus Christ, the Head, through membership in the Catholic Church, which is His Mystical Body. The Catholic Church alone possesses the means of salvation (the Seven Sacraments and the infallible Magisterium), and both Christ and the Catholic Church are necessary for salvation. Of course, this does not

9

mean non-Catholics have no chance to be saved. If some-
one is invincibly ignorant of the need to be a member
of the Catholic Church and seeks God with a sincere
heart, he may still have the possibility of salvation, by
God's grace.[1] That is, there may be a way in which he
can "invisibly" be inside the Catholic Church (in which
case he would not truly be a "non-Catholic"). God does
not punish those who are not guilty of deliberate sin.
God's mercy is as infinite as His justice.

Nevertheless, although the salvation of such a person may be a possibility, this does not necessarily mean
a "probability" or even a "good possibility." The possibility may be quite remote. In light of this reality,
Catholics must hold to what they know with certainty:
*A person must enter the Catholic Church through Bap-
tism in order to be saved.*[2] Jesus said, "Amen, amen I
say to thee, unless a man be born again of water and
the Holy Ghost, he cannot enter into the kingdom of
God" (*John* 3:5); "He that believes and is baptized shall
be saved, but he that believeth not will be condemned."
(*Mark* 16:16). Our Lord also warned us: "Enter ye in
at the narrow gate, for wide is the gate and broad is
the way that leads to destruction, and many there are
who go in thereat. How narrow is the gate and strait
is the way that leads to life, and few there are that
find it." (*Matthew* 7:13-14). For these reasons, Blessed
Pius IX condemned the idea that "Good hope at least
is to be entertained of the eternal salvation of all those
who are not at all in the true Church of Christ."[3]
Masonry denies the divine truth that the Catholic
Church is the one way of salvation, since it advances
its members to the "heavenly lodge above" regardless
of their individual religious beliefs.

Freemasonry's Teachings Come from Enlightenment Thinking

Masonry's belief that all men are saved was influenced by the Enlightenment period, in the late 18th century, when modern Freemasonry's rituals were established. The Enlightenment was a period marked by a desire to free mankind from the "oppression" of religious dogma and the authority of the Catholic Church. Instead of submitting to the supernatural truths that God has revealed through Scripture and Apostolic Tradition, Enlightenment thinkers pursued the knowledge of God solely through the rational study of nature. Man was to use his intellect to determine the truth that he would follow. While these rationalists maintained a generic faith in God, they discarded the revealed truths of Adam's Fall, Original Sin, Grace and Redemption through Jesus Christ.

The modern rituals of Freemasonry reflect the rationalism of Enlightenment thinking. Masonic ritual teaches Masons "to pay that rational homage to Deity"[4] and refers to "geometry" and the "five human senses" as gateways to the knowledge of God.[5] As we will see, Masonry uses the letter *G* as a symbol for "God" and "Geometry."[6] The Masonic Service Association, which was organized by Masons to educate the public about Freemasonry, even claims that "Geometry provides the nearest possible 'proof' of His existence."[7] Geometry is thus considered "the basis on which the superstructure of Masonry is erected."[8]

Freemasonry Is a Religion of Naturalism

While Freemasonry professes a *natural* belief in a supreme being, it holds that the *supernatural* truths of the Blessed Trinity, the Incarnation of the Son of God, the atoning death of Jesus Christ, the necessity of the Sacraments for salvation, and anything else uniquely Catholic are relative and dispensable. Even though Christ has revealed the truths of salvation in Scripture and Tradition, as authoritatively interpreted by His Church, Masonry claims that "No man can put such things into words, much less into hard and fast dogma."[9] Masonry's view of Revelation was condemned by the First Vatican Council: "If anyone says that it is impossible, or not expedient, that human beings should be taught by means of divine Revelation, let him be anathema."[10]

To gain the spiritual benefits of Freemasonry, a Mason must profess only a rational "belief in deity" and in some kind of life everlasting, without regard for specific religious beliefs. To enter into the "heavenly lodge above," the Mason need not believe in the Lord and Saviour Jesus Christ or in any divine revelation. While a "Christian" Mason may privately believe in Jesus, Masonry requires no such belief, because the Mason already "has within him the sure foundation of eternal life."[11]

Because of its exclusively naturalistic approach to God, the Popes have called Freemasonry a religion of "Naturalism."[12] *Naturalism* looks upon reason as the fundamental source of all truth and seeks to explain everything in the world in terms of humanly understandable causes. In his condemnation of Freemasonry, Pope Leo XIII defined Naturalism as the denial of any "dogma of religion or truth which cannot be understood by the human intelligence."[13] Pope Leo XIII accused those who would "substitute Naturalism for Christianity and the worship of reason for the worship of faith" of having "satanic intent."[14]

Freemasonry Deceives its Members with Christian-sounding Terminology

As we will see, Freemasonry colors its Naturalism with a few dashes of Catholicism by using terms like *rebirth, enlightenment* and *resurrection.* This technique is employed to deceive Catholics. As Albert Pike, the father of Scottish Rite Freemasonry, admits, Masonry "uses false explanations and misinterpretations of its symbols to *mislead* those who deserve only to be misled; to *conceal* the Truth, which it calls Light, from them, and to draw them away from it."[15] Martin Wagner, a scholar of Freemasonry, explains that the Lodge uses Christian terminology "not to express the Christian ideas or to show their harmony with Christian thought, but to give them a Christian coloring, the more effectually to *deceive, mislead and hoodwink* the neophyte, the conscientious member and the non-Mason."[16]

Masonry's deceptive use of Christian expressions and symbolism fits in with a world view which is also at the heart of Modernist thinking. *Modernism* seeks to update the unchanging truths of the Catholic Faith with ideas of modern man. These ideas include the Rationalism and Naturalism promoted by Freemasonry. By retaining certain elements of the Faith as a veneer for their novel theology, Modernists "cover certain principles of Catholic doctrine, so as to wrap them in the obscurity of oblivion."[17]

In his condemnation of Modernism, Pope St. Pius X observed how the Modernist mix of Rationalism and Catholicism is used to deceive the Faithful and lead souls to ruin: "Further, none is more skillful, none more astute than they, in the employment of a thousand noxious arts; for they *play the double role of rationalist and Catholic*—and this so craftly that they easily lead the unwary into error."[18] This canonized Pope called Modernism "the synthesis of all heresies."[19] Many Catholics easily ingest the Rationalist errors of Masonry when they see them couched in familiar Catholic terms like *God, soul, resurrection* and *heaven.*

Freemasonry Views Catholicism As "Sectarian"

Freemasonry calls any religious belief outside of its system of Naturalism a "sectarian" belief. *Sectarian* is a derogatory term that is used to label individual religions as limited and even divisive. For example, the Catholic teachings on the Eucharist—truths which a Catholic must die for rather than deny—are considered *sectarian* beliefs, that is, denominational peculiarities of the Catholic Church which place a barrier between Catholics and non-Catholics. As Joseph Fort Newton explains, "Masonry seeks to free men from a limited conception of religion, and thus to remove one of the chief causes of sectarianism."[20] Mackey also tells us that the "religion of freemasonry is not sectarian. It admits men of every creed within its hospitable bosom, rejecting none and approving none for his particular faith. It is not Judaism . . . it is not Christianity."[21]

Because the religious doctrines of Freemasonry are "very simple and self-evident," they are not darkened by "perplexities of sectarian theology," but are "acceptable by all minds, for they ask only for a belief in God and in the immortality of the soul."[22] All men, "whether they have received their teachings from Confucius, Zoroaster, Moses, Mohammed or the founder of the Christian religion," can worship at the altar of Freemasonry as they journey to eternal life with God.[23] (Notice the omission of any reference to "Jesus" or "Christ.")

Freemasonry Promotes the Heresy of Indifferentism

Holding that the dogmatic truths of the Catholic Faith are superfluous and sectarian is a heresy known as *Indifferentism.* Indifferentism holds that all religions are legitimate paths to God. Pope Pius XI explained that Indifferentism "considers all religions to be more or less good and praiseworthy, since they all, in different ways, manifest and signify that sense which is inborn in us all and by which we are led to God and to the obedient acknowledgement of His rule."[24] Pope Gregory XVI declared "Indifferentism" to be "another abundant source of the evils with which the Church is afflicted at present."[25]

Blessed Pius IX called Indifferentism "a very grave error entrapping some Catholics, who believe that it is possible to arrive at eternal salvation although living in error and alienated from the True Faith and Catholic unity."[26] Pope Leo XIII even labeled Indifferentism "a rashness unknown to the very pagans."[27] Our Lord also revealed His rejection of those who espouse the lukewarmness of Indifferentism: "I know thy works, that thou art neither cold nor hot. I would that thou wert cold or hot. But because thou art lukewarm, and neither cold nor hot, I will begin to vomit thee out of my mouth." (*Apocalypse* 3:15-16).

Indifferentism seeks to destroy especially the Catholic religion, "the only one that is true." Pope Leo XIII said:

> Again, as all who offer themselves [to Masonry] are received, whatever may be their form of religion, they [the Masons] thereby teach the great error of this age—that a regard for religion should be held as an indifferent

matter, and that all religions are alike. This
manner of reasoning is calculated to bring
about the ruin of all forms of religion, and
especially of the Catholic religion, which, as
it is the only one that is true, cannot without great injustice be regarded as merely equal
to other religions.[28]

Pope Pius XI also explains that Indifferentism leads
to Naturalism, which can ultimately lead a person to
atheism: "Not only are those who hold this opinion in
error and deceived; but also, in distorting the idea of
true religion, they reject it, and little by little turn aside
to Naturalism and atheism, as it is called; from which
it clearly follows that one who supports those who hold
these theories and attempt to realize them is altogether
abandoning the divinely revealed religion."[29]

Masonry Allies Itself with Satan

Indifferentism is a grave insult to God and an offense
against His divine justice. St. Paul reveals that God
wills "all men to be saved and to come to the knowledge of the truth." (*1 Timothy* 2:4). In order to effect
His desire, God revealed Himself in the Person of Jesus
Christ, who died for our sins and established a Church
"which he has purchased with his own blood." (*Acts*
20:28). Just as Jesus Christ has redeemed us through
the sacrifice of His physical body, He applies the fruits
of His Redemption to us through His Mystical Body,
the Roman Catholic Church.[30] As St. Paul says in his
Letter to the *Ephesians,* Jesus is the Saviour of His
Body, the Church. (See *Ephesians* 5:23.)

Those who treat Jesus Christ and membership in
His Church as sectarian and as unnecessary innova-

tions seek to undermine God's plan of salvation and divert souls to Hell. Such people have "changed the truth of God into a lie." (*Romans* 1:25). Thus, the teachings of Freemasonry are from the devil, who is the father of lies. "When he speaketh a lie, he speaketh of his own, for he is a liar and the father thereof." (*John* 8:44). As Bl. Pius IX warned, "For from these [Masonic lodges], the synagogue of Satan is formed, which draws up its forces, advances its standards, and joins battle against the Church of Christ."[31]

Now that we have some background, let us examine the errors and practices of Freemasonry in more detail. As we shall see, Masonry not only promotes the error of Indifferentism, it goes *beyond* Indifferentism by advancing its *own* unique doctrines about God and eternal life. We shall present this material by examining what happens in the lodge room during a man's initiation into Freemasonry. We shall consider the pertinent parts of all three degrees, with an emphasis on the initiation rite of the First Degree. Since I have received these degrees and have conferred them many times, my approach provides the reader with a unique perspective that he may not find elsewhere.

—4—
Preparation for the
First Degree

When a man arrives at the Masonic Temple or Lodge to receive the First Degree of Freemasonry, the Degree of Entered Apprentice, he is escorted to a private room. He is first commanded to lay aside all thought of levity and address his mind to the solemn truths he is about to learn. He is then told to strip down to his underwear. In addition to his clothing, the candidate is required to remove all jewelry, including his wedding ring, crucifix, scapular, and any other sacramental that he might be wearing. He later learns that he was divested of his religious reminders so that he might "carry nothing offensive or defensive into the lodge."[1]

While some Masons claim that Freemasonry encourages a man to practice his own faith, Freemasonry actually requires the candidate to divest himself of all reminders of his faith—an obvious and blatant contradiction of this claim. The candidate for Freemasonry cannot have any "sectarian" articles about him as he receives the religious "truths" of the Lodge. Ho must remove even his wedding ring; this requirement is particularly noteworthy, for a Catholic man's wedding ring symbolizes not only the indissoluble sacramental union between him and his bride but also the indissoluble union between Jesus Christ and the Catholic Church. (See *Ephesians* 5:23-32). After the candidate complies with this requirement, he is blindfolded with a "hoodwink" and secured with a noose called a "cabletow" around his neck. In this state of helplessness, the candidate is prepared to receive the "truths" of Freemasonry and is conducted to the Inner Door of the Lodge.

—5—

Spiritual Darkness

The Christian Candidate Has "Long Been in Darkness"

At the Inner Door, the candidate knocks three times. The Senior Deacon opens the door and asks, "Who comes here?" The Junior Deacon responds for the candidate: "Mr. _____, who has long been in darkness, and now seeks to be brought to light."[1] Even though the candidate has been blindfolded for just a few minutes, the Junior Deacon declares that he has *long* been in darkness." Freemasonry is clear that the candidate's darkness refers not just to his ignorance of a few fraternity passwords *but to his current spiritual condition.* The *Masonic Bible* teaches:

> darkness is a symbol of *ignorance*; while light is the symbol of enlightenment and knowledge. It is a principle of Freemasonry that the natural eye cannot perceive of the mysteries of the Order until the heart has embraced the *deep spiritual and mystic meanings* of those sublime mysteries. Hence, all applicants for the Degrees of Freemasonry are required to enter the Lodge in total darkness; this dark-

ness is preparatory and preliminary to his receiving the light he desires and searches.[2]

Even though the Christian candidate has been baptized into the light of Jesus Christ—thereby receiving *Sanctifying Grace,* which is a created sharing in the very life of God, making the recipient a *child of God;* as well as thereby receiving the *virtue of faith,* which enables him to believe all the truths revealed by God; plus receiving in Baptism other *supernatural virtues (powers) and gifts;* not to mention the fact that Baptism actually makes him an *heir of Heaven*—Masonry nevertheless declares that he is in a state of spiritual and mystical darkness. The candidate must die to his former life in Christ and be reborn into the new life of the Lodge. It is his initiation into Freemasonry, and not Christian Baptism, that makes the Mason a "son of light."[3] As Allen Roberts explains to Masons in his popular book on Freemasonry, *The Craft and Its Symbols,* "Your preparation for your entrance into Freemasonry began the day your mother brought you into the world. Your entrance into the Lodge for initiation became, symbolically, your *rebirth.*"[4] Mackey further explains the spiritual, moral and intellectual deficiencies of the uninitiated:

> Having been wandering amid the *errors* and covered over with the pollutions of the outer and profane world, he comes inquiringly to our doors, seeking the *new birth*, and asking a withdrawal of the veil which conceals *divine truth from his uninitiated sight* . . . There is to be, not simply a change for the future, but also an extinction of the past . . . the chains

of *error and ignorance* which have previously
restrained the candidate in *moral and intellectual* captivity are broken.[5]

Freemasonry Denies the Light of Jesus Christ

It should offend any Catholic to be declared to be
in a state of spiritual darkness. Jesus Christ said, "I
am the light of the world; he that follows me walketh
not in darkness, but shall have the light of life." (*John*
8:12).[6] Contrary to what Masonry teaches, those who
are baptized into Christ have been "called out of darkness into his marvelous light." (*1 Peter* 2:9). By receiving the virtue of faith at Baptism they have been
enabled to believe in the Blessed Trinity, the Incarnation, the Holy Eucharist, Sanctifying Grace, and all
other Catholic teachings. Men are "born again" not
through their initiation into Freemasonry, but by "water
and the Spirit." (*John* 3:5).[7] Baptism is the true "illu-
mination" and "enlightenment."[8] Thus, as members of
Christ's Mystical Body, Christians are no longer slaves
of darkness, but "children of light" (*1 Thessalonians*
5:5)[9] and "partakers of the divine nature." (*2 Peter*
1:4).[10] Only the devil could call light darkness and
darkness light. But this should be no surprise, "For
Satan himself transforms himself into an angel of light."
(*2 Corinthians* 11:14).

After the declaration of his spiritual darkness, the
blindfolded candidate is conducted into the lodge room.
After only a few steps, the Senior Deacon presses a
knife or other sharp tool into the candidate's bare breast
and declares: "On this, your first admission into a Lodge
of Free and Accepted Masons, you are received on the

point of a sharp instrument piercing your naked left breast, which is to teach you that, as this is an instrument of torture to your flesh, so should the recollection of it be to your conscience, should you ever presume to reveal the secrets of Freemasonry unlawfully."[11]

—6—

Freemasonry's Worship of "Deity"

The Grand Architect of the Universe

After warning the candidate never to reveal the secrets of Freemasonry to the profane world, the Worshipful Master explains to the candidate that no man should ever engage in any great or important undertaking without first "invoking the blessing of deity."[1] The candidate is then conducted to the center of the lodge room and made to kneel. At this time, the candidate hears Freemasonry's petitions to the *Grand Architect of the Universe*.

While Christians are to pray "in the name of Jesus,"[2] Freemasonry deliberately omits Jesus' name from its prayers, as it calls upon the deity as the "Grand Architect" (and by other similar titles). In this way, the Lodge conditions its members to view God according to the Masonic worldview: *as the deity of any and every religious faith*. Even though Jesus' Name is above "every name that is named" (*Ephesians* 1:21), Masonry calls God the "Nameless One of an hundred names" and states that, no matter how we pray, we are "yet praying to the one God and Father of all."[3] As Masonic

24

author Manly Hall explains: To the true Mason, "Christ, Buddha, or Mohammed, the name means little."[4] Thus, Freemasonry denies that Jesus Christ is the one true God[5] and the "one mediator of God and men, the man Christ Jesus, who gave himself a redemption for all." (*1 Timothy* 2:5-6).

Freemasonry's Worship Promotes Idolatry

When St. Paul traveled to Athens, he noticed how sincere the Greeks were in their worship of pagan deities. Everywhere Paul saw shrines and objects of their worship. He even noticed an altar with the inscription "To the unknown god." (*Acts* 17:23). But St. Paul did not let the Greeks on Mars Hill remain in their ignorance. Nor did he join them in their worship of the "Nameless One of an hundred names." Instead, St. Paul called them to repent of their sins and to profess faith in Jesus Christ because of God's coming judgment on the world. (*Acts* 17:30-31). Anything less from St. Paul would have been an approval of idolatry.

It is the same in the Masonic lodge room. If the "Catholic" Mason argues that Masonic prayers are for him an act of worship of Christ, he must also admit that the Hindu sees these same prayers as worship of Brahma. Objectively speaking, since Brahma is a false god, this means the "Catholic" Mason is promoting the evil of idolatry and committing mortal sin. This is a grave offense against God and His First Commandment: "Thou shalt not have strange gods before me." (*Exodus* 20:3).

Catholic Worship with Masons
Is Prohibited

It is important to recall that the Church has always forbidden the Catholic to worship with non-Catholics. For example, Pope Pius XI declared: "So, Venerable Brethren, it is clear why this Apostolic See has never allowed its subjects to take part in the assemblies of non-Catholics: for the union of Christians can only be promoted by promoting the return to the one true Church of Christ of those who are separated from it."[6] In order to promote this desired unity, the Second Vatican Council made a pastoral exception to the Church's discipline on common prayer. In the document *Unitatis Redintegratio* (which means "restoration of unity"), the Church said it might be permissible for Catholics to pray with non-Catholic *Christians*, but only if regulated by the local bishop and for the purpose of bringing them back into communion with the Catholic Church (hence the title of the conciliar document).[7]

While this was an unprecedented exception to the Church's perennial practice, it should be noted that the Council did *not* permit Catholic prayer with *non-Christians*, particularly Freemasons. In fact, the canon law that was still in effect during Vatican II excommunicated any Catholic who joined Freemasonry, and the Council did not change this law. (More on this later.) As the *Catechism of the Catholic Church* states, "Christian prayer is a covenant relationship between God and man in Christ."[8] Only those who are reborn in the waters of Baptism enjoy this intimate, covenant relationship with God.

St. Thomas Aquinas teaches that God does not respond to the prayer of a sinner praying *as a sinner*, that is, in accord with a sinful desire. Thus, God would not respond to prayers by "Catholic" Masons for such perverted favors as blessings upon a Masonic Lodge (except that, according to St. Thomas, God sometimes hears the sinful prayer of a sinner *out of vengeance,* when He allows the sinner to fall even deeper into sin).[9]

Moreover, the prayer of a Catholic must always give witness to the truths of salvation and the unity of the Church. Freemasonry's prayers, on the other hand, obscure these truths by presenting a non-Christian spirituality as complementary to the unique mediation of Jesus Christ, an idea that is offensive to the Catholic Faith.[10]

The Church's principle of *Lex orandi, lex credendi*— "The law of prayer is the law of belief"—certainly applies here.[11] The way we pray flows from what we believe, but it also affects our understanding of what we believe. In other words, if a Catholic prays with Masons, he will begin to *believe* like a Mason, just as he will believe like a Protestant if he prays with Protestants. In either case, the Catholic confirms his fellow non-Catholics in their errors while jeopardizing his own salvation.[12]

—7—
Who Is the God
Of Freemasonry?

The Letter G

Freemasonry has not only its own names for God, but also its own symbols for God. As we have already mentioned, one of these symbols is the letter *G* (which stands for both God and Geometry). The letter *G* hangs in the eastern quadrant of the lodge room above the chair of the Worshipful Master. The newly-made Mason is directed to the letter *G* once his hoodwink is removed. The Masonic Bible says that the letter *G* "represents the great God of all Freemasons."[1] Thus, in the Fellowcraft Degree, all Masons *bow in worship* before the letter *G*.[2] As Manly Hall explains, a true Mason is one who "worships at every shrine, bows before every altar, whether in temple, mosque or cathedral, realizing . . . the oneness of all spiritual truth."[3]

The All-Seeing Eye

Another of Masonry's symbols for God is the All-Seeing Eye, which has clear connections to Enlightenment Deism. Deists, like all rationalists, reject revealed truth and religious authority in favor of intellectual speculation about God. Deists view God as the

All-Seeing Eye, who, after creating the world, no longer takes an active role in its course. Coil claims that the All-Seeing Eye was used by the pagan Egyptians to represent the god Osiris.[4] The Masonic Service Association boasts that the symbol pre-dates Christianity by a thousand years.[5] The symbol of the All-Seeing Eye is displayed on Masonic aprons, typically those worn by Past Worshipful Masters.

Incidentally, although ancient paganism can be said, in a certain sense, to "pre-date" Christianity, the Christian religion actually goes all the way back to Adam through the Old Testament, by which God was preparing the world for Jesus Christ and the Christian religion. Thus, the origins of the Christian religion pre-date all pagan religions.

Freemasonry Promotes the Error of Syncretism

Masonry's use of the letter *G* and the All-Seeing Eye facilitates its syncretistic understanding of deity. *Syncretism* is the deliberate blending of different beliefs or practices, without regard to their compatibility with Christian truth. Syncretism is the logical consequence of Indifferentism, for if all religions are equal, there is no problem with mingling them together. By using unique names and symbols that are not particular to any individual religion, Masonry not only unites men of different faiths into one spiritual brotherhood, but also unites the deities of different religions *into one spiritual godhead*. The *Masonic Bible* calls this monstrous syncretism the "unity of the Godhead."[6]

Freemasonry's symbolism and nomenclature go beyond promoting a deistic understanding of God, even to embracing a polytheistic understanding of deity. In fact, Coil says that monotheism "violates Masonic principles, for it requires belief in a specific kind of Supreme Deity."[7] Oliver Street, another Masonic author, states that Masons could embrace not only "pantheism, nature religions and animism," but also nature worship, polytheism, fetishism, and sorcery.[8]

Presumably, most American Masons are monotheists. On this basis, some Masons may wish to defend the "monotheism" of the Lodge. However, Hindus, Buddhists, Shintoists and other polytheists may also be members of Freemasonry because they "believe in deity." Masonry does not limit its membership to Christians, Jews and Muslims. Moreover, even if Masonry promoted monotheism (it does not), the Lodge would still regard a Deistic or Unitarian understanding of God as an equally acceptable alternative to the truth of the Blessed Trinity.

In the final analysis, The Grand Architect of the Universe of the Masonic Lodge is *not* the Holy Trinity, and therefore, *it is a false god*. Thus, Masonry's teachings and practices are an abomination before the one true God—the Father, Son and Holy Ghost, as revealed by Jesus Christ—and Catholics must have nothing to do with them. As St. Paul says, Although there are many so-called "gods" and "lords" in heaven and on earth, "yet to us there is but one God, the Father, of whom are all things, and we unto him; and one Lord Jesus Christ, by whom are all things, and we by him." (*1 Corinthians* 8:5-6).

—8—

Freemasonry's Profession of Faith in the Deity

"In Whom Do You Put Your Trust?"

After the Worshipful Master prays to the Grand Architect of the Universe, he places his hand upon the kneeling candidate's head and asks, "In whom do you put your trust?"[1] If the candidate responds with a profession of faith in *any* "supreme deity," the Worshipful Master declares to him: "Your trust being in God, your faith is well-founded. Arise, follow your conductor, and fear no danger."[2]

No matter what "God" the candidate professes, Masonry assures him that his trust is *in God* and his faith is *well-founded*. Thus, for those candidates who reject Jesus Christ, *Freemasonry lies to them*. No matter how erroneous their beliefs, the Lodge tells these Masons that they have the truth. In Masonry, there is no such thing as a false god. As Past Grand Master Carl Claudy explains, "A hundred paths may wind upward around a mountain; at the top they meet."[3] The *Masonic Bible* also says that "Freemasonry reverences all titles by which God is known."[4]

31

Freemasonry's View of God Is Contrary to Reason

Freemasonry's teaching about God is contrary not only to His Revelation through Jesus Christ, but to reason as well. If two Masons have incompatible beliefs about God and one of them is true, the other one must necessarily be false. Therefore, the erroneous belief of the second person cannot be "well-founded." To hold the beliefs of both Masons to be true, as Masonry does, is to violate reason and to deny objective truth altogether. The Masonic Service Association even says, "One of the greatest truths man has learned, in all his centuries of study, is that there is no absolute to be known; all truths, including the mathematical, are relative."[5] Such an argument, besides being incompatible with Catholic belief, is self-defeating—and also self-contradictory, because this Masonic principle is itself considered an absolute truth in the Masonic belief system, and therefore there *is* an absolute in the Lodge, despite what Masonry says.

About Masonic Indifferentism, Bl. Pius IX stated, "Without doubt, nothing more insane than such a doctrine, nothing more impious or more opposed to reason itself could be devised."[6] Pope Pius VIII also declared that "this deadly idea concerning the lack of difference among religions is refuted even by the light of natural reason. We are assured of this because the various religions do not often agree among themselves. If one is true, the other must be false; there can be no society of darkness with light."[7] St. Paul warns us:

> Bear not the yoke with unbelievers. For what participation hath justice with injustice? Or what fellowship hath light with darkness? And

what concord hath Christ with Belial? Or what part hath the faithful with the unbeliever? And what agreement hath the temple of God with idols? For you are the temple of the living God; as God saith: *I will dwell in them, and walk among them; and I will be their God, and they shall be my people.* Wherefore, *"Go out from among them, and be ye separate,"* saith the Lord, and touch not the unclean thing. (*2 Corinthians* 6:14-17).

—9—

Freemasonry's Oaths

The Candidate Swears a Curse upon Himself

After the candidate professes his faith, he is conducted around the lodge room. He is then instructed to approach the Masonic altar, which Masonry calls a "place of sacrifice."[1] As the candidate stands blindfolded before the altar, the Worshipful Master informs him that he is required to take a solemn and binding oath. The Worshipful Master assures the candidate that there is nothing in the oath that will conflict with any duty he owes to God, country, neighbor or self. The candidate is then caused to kneel at the altar and place his hands in a particular way upon the Volume of the Sacred Law (which, if the candidate is a Christian, is the holy Bible).

The term "place of sacrifice" is very appropriate because the candidate at the altar 1) swears blood-oaths and 2) sacrifices his former religious faith for the new religious faith of Freemasonry. In each of the three Masonic oaths, the candidate swears he will conform his life to the teachings of Freemasonry. The candidate swears never to reveal Masonry's secrets to profanes. The candidate also swears a curse upon himself, that he would be worthy of a grisly death if he ever violated his oath. For example, the candidate swears that he would be worthy "Of having my throat cut across, my tongue torn out and with my body buried in the sands of the sea";[2] "Of having my left breast torn open, my heart plucked out and placed on the highest pinnacle of the temple";[3] "Of having my body severed in twain, my bowels taken thence and burned to ashes, the ashes scattered to the four winds of heaven";[4] and, "Of having my eyeballs pierced to the center with a three-inch blade, my feet flayed, and forced to walk the hot sands of the sterile shores of the Red Sea."[5]

Freemasonry's Oaths Violate the Second Commandment

The Church condemns these oaths as a violation of the Second Commandment because they use God's holy name in vain. An oath must not be taken for purposes contrary to "ecclesial communion:[6] (union with the Church), such as to make a commitment to Freemasonry. As Father Heribert Jone states in his classic work, *Moral Theology,* "To promise something evil under oath is mortally sinful, at least if the thing promised be gravely sinful."[7] To join Freemasonry is gravely sinful (see p. 54 below); therefore, swearing a Masonic oath is a mortal sin.

It should be noted that an oath to do something sinful is not morally binding. "No obligation arises from an oath to do something that is forbidden or useless."[8] (Nevertheless, such an oath must be confessed in the Sacrament of Penance. See Appendix D.) It is also a sin to fulfill a sinful oath.

Furthermore, God's name must never be used for inappropriate or trivial matters. For example, the

candidate swears not to reveal Masonry's trivial passwords and secret handshakes to non-Masons. Invoking God's name over such frivolous matters constitutes
rash swearing, which compounds the gravity of the
sin.[9] The candidate also swears that he will not "cheat,
wrong or defraud" a brother Mason or a lodge of
Masons.[10] Since we are already bound by God's laws
not to do all these things and also to *love* our neighbor, this is an idle and unnecessary use of God's name.

The candidate further swears that he will not "have
illicit carnal intercourse with a Master Mason's wife,
mother, sister or daughter."[11] This promise is not only
unnecessary because God and the natural law already
condemn fornication and adultery, it is also gravely
offensive to pious ears. If the Church does not require
Catholics to swear oaths promising to avoid sins of
impurity, Masonry has no reason to do so. For all these
reasons, the Masonic oath contitutes blasphemy—a
grave sin against God and His Holy Name.[12] Pope Benedict XIV called the Masonic oath contrary to the laws
of the state and of religion,[13] and Pope Leo XII declared
it "abominable," "impious" and "accursed."[14]

What about Fraternal Pledges?

Many people ask about the difference between the
Masonic oaths and the pledges taken by Catholic fraternal orders such as the Knights of Columbus. There
are a number of significant differences. First, because
the Masonic oath uses the formulae, "I swear to God"
and "so help me God," it formally calls upon God to
witness the promise. Fraternal pledges, on the other
hand, do not call God to formally witness the promise—
which is why they are pledges and not oaths. The pledge-
giver says, "I give you my word" (not "I swear to God").

Second, fraternal pledges, such as those required in the Knights of Columbus, are read to the candidate in advance. This is done so that the candidate fully realizes what he is promising. In Freemasonry, the oaths are *not* read to the candidate in advance. The Worshipful Master simply assures the candidate that the oath will not conflict with his religious duties, even though the Master usually has no idea about the candidate's religious beliefs.

Third, the Masonic oaths not only include condemnable self-curses, but Masons are required to simulate these curses with various hand gestures (called "Signs") at every lodge meeting. For example, when giving the Entered Apprentice Sign, the Mason moves his right hand across his neck to imitate the slitting of his throat. The Fellowcraft Sign requires the Mason to move his hand across his chest to simulate plucking out his heart. In the Master Mason Sign, the Mason moves his hand across his waist to indicate severing his body to remove his bowels. All Masons are required to make these signs throughout Masonic ritual and when addressing the Worshipful Master.

Finally and most obviously, the pledges of Catholic fraternal orders like the Knights of Columbus are meant to inspire the candidate to deepen his relationship with Jesus Christ and the Church. The Masonic oaths do just the opposite. Thus, the pledges of fraternities like the Knights of Columbus and the oaths of the Masons are as radically different as is their theology. For those "Catholic" Masons who would rather give an affirmation rather than swear an oath to God, the *Masonic Bible* says, "Affirmations instead of oaths are entirely inadmissible in Freemasonry."[15]

—10—
Freemasonry's View Of the Holy Bible

The Bible Is Only a Symbol

After the candidate swears the Masonic oath, the Worshipful Master asks the candidate what he most desires. The candidate is prompted to say, "Light." After the candidate answers, the Worshipful Master declares to the Lodge that he will now bring the newly made brother "from darkness to light." After reciting the first three verses of the creation account in the *Book of Genesis*, the Worshipful Master says, "Let there be light!"[1] At this point, the Mason's hoodwink is removed and he finds himself kneeling at the Masonic altar. He also finds his hands resting upon the Volume of the Sacred Law and on the Square and Compass. (If the candidate is a Christian, the Volume of the Sacred Law for him is the Holy Bible.) These three, the Worshipful Master now explains, are the "Three Great Lights in Masonry."[2]

While Freemasonry calls the Holy Bible one of the Three Great Lights, it views the Bible as *only a symbol* of God's revelation or will, just like the Square and Compass that rest on top of it. Because the Bible contains God's supernatural revelation, Masonry's religion of Naturalism must reject it as an authority. Coil says that "the Bible is only a symbol of Divine Will, Law or Revelation" and adds that "no responsible authority has held that a Freemason must believe the Bible or any part of it."[3] "In fact," says Masonic author George Chase Wingate, "Blue Lodge Masonry has *nothing whatsoever* to do with the Bible; it is not founded on the Bible. If it was, it would not be Masonry; it would be something else."[4]

Other Religious Writings Are Equal to the Bible

Just as Freemasonry views all gods as equal to the Blessed Trinity, it views all religious writings as equal to the Bible. The Masonic Service Association tells us, "Whether it be the Gospels of the Christian, the Book of Law of the Hebrew, the Koran of the Mussulman, or the Vedas of the Hindu, it [the Volume of the Sacred Law] everywhere Masonically conveys the same idea—symbolizing the will of God revealed to man."[5] Thus, Coil explains that "whatever to any people expresses that will may be used as a substitute for the Bible in a Masonic Lodge."[6] When a Muslim is initiated into the Lodge, the *Koran* becomes the "Great Light of Masonry." When a Zoroastrian is initiated, the *Zend Avesta* is the Great Light. It is the same with the *Talmud,* the *Book of Mormon,* the *Vedas,* the *Sohar,* the *Bhagavad Gita,* the *Upanishads,* and any other writing considered sacred by the religion of the initiate. All are legitimate substitutes for the written Word of God.

Masonry's view of the Bible as a replaceable symbol of the revelation and will of God is repugnant to the Catholic Faith. The Church teaches that *"God is the author of Sacred Scripture.* The divinely revealed realities, which are contained and presented in the text of Sacred Scripture, have been written down under the inspiration of the Holy Ghost."[7] In fact, the Church has always taught that the books of Scripture were dictated to the sacred authors by the Holy Ghost.[8] Pope Leo XIII affirmed the same in his famous encyclical on the study of Holy Scripture: "For all the books which the Church receives as sacred and canonical are written wholly and entirely, with all their parts, at the dictation of the Holy Ghost. This is the ancient and unchanging faith of the Church."[9]

As with its view of God, Masonry's view of the Bible is contrary both to Revelation and to reason. To Freemasonry, it does not matter that the Bible affirms the divinity of Christ, whereas the Koran denies His divinity. To the Lodge, *both* views, however contradictory, express the "will of God." Only the Father of Lies could have contrived such a damnable idea.

—11—

Freemasonry's Salvation
By Works

The Masonic Apron

After the Mason is taught about the Three Great
Lights, the Worshipful Master presents him with his
lambskin or white leathern apron. The Masonic apron
is called the "badge" of a Mason and is worn around
the waist at all official Masonic gatherings. As he presents the apron to the new Mason, the Worshipful Master introduces him to the Lodge's belief in salvation
by works, independent of God's gift of grace through
Jesus Christ:

> The lamb has in all ages been deemed an
> emblem of innocence; he, therefore, who wears
> the lambskin as a badge of Masonry is thereby
> continually reminded of that *purity of life and
> conduct*, which is *essentially necessary to his
> gaining admission into the Celestial Lodge
> above*, where the Supreme Architect of the
> Universe presides.[1]

41

The Masonic Jewels and Common Gavel

The Worshipful Master also teaches the Entered Apprentice about the three immovable and three movable jewels of the Lodge. The immovable jewels are the Square, the Level and the Plumb, which, respectively, teach morality, equality and rectitude of conduct. The movable jewels are the Rough Ashlar, the Perfect Ashlar and the Trestleboard. Masons are taught that the Rough Ashlar represents their "rude and imperfect state by nature"; the Perfect Ashlar represents the "state of perfection at which we hope to arrive"; and the Trestleboard is the instrument by which Masons are to "erect our spiritual building."[2]

So that he can reach the desired state of perfection before God, the Worshipful Master presents the Entered Apprentice with a "Common Gavel," explaining:

> The Common Gavel is an instrument made use of by operative Masons to break off the corners of rough stones, the better to fit them for the builder's use; but we as Free and Accepted Masons are taught to make use of it for the more noble and glorious purpose of divesting our minds and consciences of the vices and superfluities of life, thereby fitting us as *living stones for that spiritual building, that house not made with hands, eternal in the heavens.*[3]

Through its symbolic use of the Rough Ashlar, Perfect Ashlar, Trestleboard and Common Gavel and its repeated references to "conduct" and "morality," Freemasonry teaches that a Mason's works will get him to heaven, *no matter what religion he professes*. Masonry's moralization of religion makes the Catholic Faith nothing more than an optional system of ethical behavior, useful for helping one lead a better life, but not the exclusive means by which God saves man from the fires of Hell.

In his encyclical condemning Indifferentism, Pope Gregory XVI said that "This perverse opinion is spread on all sides by the fraud of the wicked, who claim that it is possible to obtain the eternal salvation of the soul by the profession of any kind of religion, *as long as morality is maintained*. Surely, in so clear a matter, you will drive this deadly error far from the people committed to your care."[4]

Freemasonry Rejects the Catholic Church's Teaching on Grace

Masonry's notion that man can gain Heaven by practicing his own version of morality is irreconcilable with the Catholic Faith, not only because it views Catholic morality as relative, but also because it denies any need for the Saviour or for His Church. The Catholic Church teaches that prior to repentance and Baptism, man is separated from God and is under the curse of eternal death for the sin of Adam.[5] Man is born under the condemnation "of the law." (*Romans* 4:15; *Galatians* 3:10). There is absolutely nothing a man can do by his own efforts (whether it be by faith or by works) without Sanctifying Grace in his soul to merit eternal life. The Council of Trent teaches: "If anyone says that man can be justified before God by his own works, whether done by his own natural powers or through the teaching of the law, without divine grace through Jesus Christ, let him be anathema."[6]

It is only through the "Second Adam"—Jesus Christ—
that a man is saved from the condemnation of the law.[7]
In Baptism, God removes the "stain" of Adam's sin
(Original Sin), forgives a man his personal sins, infuses
his soul with Sanctifying Grace, by which he is "justified," and he becomes a child of God.[8] A man is then
able to have a supernatural relationship with God, and
God will reward him for his faith and works that are
performed in the state of Sanctifying Grace. If a man
does not respond to God's grace through Christ, he
remains alienated from God and can have no hope of
eternal life.[9] This is why Our Lord says, "He that
believes in him [Jesus Christ] is not judged. But he
that does not believe is *already* judged, because he
believes not in the name of the only begotten Son of
God." (*John* 3:18, emphasis added).

God is able to offer man grace to save his soul because
of the propitiatory sacrifice of Jesus Christ offered once
on Calvary and renewed in the Holy Mass.[10] Grace is
not earned by living a life of Masonic virtue, but is
given freely by God through Christ to enable us to
respond to His love.[11] Because it is God's free choice
to associate man with the work of His grace, no one
can merit the first reception of Sanctifying Grace, no
matter how "good" or "moral" he is on the natural,
human level.[12] Perfection and salvation come not by
way of the Common Gavel, but by the cross of Our
Lord Jesus Christ. Without Christ, there is no grace,
and without grace, there is no salvation. In light of
the pronouncements of the Council of Trent, Masonry's
teachings on the salvation of man without the grace
of Christ are *anathema*.

—12—

Freemasonry's Doctrine of Resurrection of the Body

The Hiramic Legend of the Third Degree

The Third Degree of Freemasonry (the degree of Master Mason) teaches the most sublime of all Masonic doctrines: the resurrection of the body and the immortality of the soul. The instruction that the Mason has received up to this point concerning the building of his "future moral and Masonic edifice"[1] culminates in this degree. The *Masonic Bible* states: "The doctrine of the *resurrection of the body* to a future and eternal life constitutes an essential dogma of the religious faith of Freemasonry. It is more authoritatively inculcated in the symbolism of the Third Degree than is possible by any dogmatic creed."[2]

Like Masonry's other teachings, the doctrine of the resurrection is conveyed through symbolism. But unlike the other teachings, where symbols are briefly explained to the candidate, the resurrection doctrine is taught by an extensive allegorical drama in which the candidate is made to participate. This drama is called the "Hiramic Legend" because the candidate plays the part of a stonemason named Hiram Abif. According to the

legend, Hiram was the master workman on King
Solomon's Temple who held the secrets of a Master
Mason. In Freemasonry, Hiram Abif is essentially
equivalent to a saviour.[3]

The legend commences with the candidate being
blindfolded and brought to kneel at the Masonic altar.
After a short prayer, the Senior Deacon helps the candidate rise and escorts him about the lodge room (which
now represents King Solomon's Temple). During his
journey, the candidate is confronted by three ruffians—
Jubela, Jubelo and Jubelum—who seek unlawfully to
procure from him the secrets of a Master Mason. After
the candidate's refusal to disclose the secrets, Jubelum
gives the candidate the "death blow" by striking his
head with a padded mallet. The candidate is knocked
off his feet and caught in a large sack by his Masonic
brothers. (The candidate is told to remain lying down.)

After the ruffians recognize the horrid deed they
have committed, they bury Hiram's body. Back at the
Temple, King Solomon, played by the Worshipful Master, recognizes Hiram's absence and dispatches a search
party of Fellowcrafts to find him. After they discover
Hiram's dead body, they inform King Solomon, who
orders a procession to Hiram's grave (at this point the
candidate's hoodwink is removed). When the Masons
reach the grave, they cry out in horror and surprise.
King Solomon orders Hiram's body to be raised, but
due to its rotting flesh, this is not possible. At this
point, the Masons kneel around the grave and the Worshipful Master says a prayer for Hiram's "everlasting
salvation."[4] The Worshipful Master then raises the candidate "from a dead level to a living perpendicular" by
the strong grip of a Master Mason.

Freemasonry's Explanation of the Hiramic Legend

The *Masonic Bible* describes the raising of the candidate as follows: "Literally, this refers to a portion of the ceremony; but more significantly, it refers symbolically to the *resurrection,* which is exemplified as the object of the degree."[5] Right after the Mason is raised, the Worshipful Master explains that the Hiramic Legend "testifies to our faith in the *resurrection of the body* and the immortality of the soul."[6] The legend concludes by repeating the teachings of the Entered Apprentice degree concerning salvation by human good conduct and not by God's grace:

> Then let us imitate the *good man* in his *virtuous and amiable conduct;* in his unfeigned piety to God; in his inflexible fidelity to his trust; that we may welcome the grim tyrant Death, and receive him as a kind messenger sent from our Supreme Grand Master, *to translate us from this imperfect to that all-perfect, glorious and celestial Lodge above,* where the Supreme Architect of the universe presides.[7]

Whereas Catholics are to pick up their cross and follow Jesus Christ, Masons are to follow the example of Hiram Abif.[8] While the Church teaches that we will receive an incorruptible and glorified body through the power of Jesus Christ's Resurrection, the Lodge says that resurrection comes about by the example of Hiram's resurrection.[9] While the Church requires faith in Jesus Christ, who is "the resurrection and the life" (*John* 11:25)—as well as Sanctifying Grace, which

entails obedience to God and to His Catholic Church—
Masonry imposes no such conditions. This is why Pope
Leo XIII called Freemasonry "the implacable enemy of
Christ and of the Church."[10] The *Masonic Bible* fur-
ther teaches:

- "Foremost of all the truths taught and emphasized
  in [the Master Mason] degree is the immortality of
  the soul of man and the certainty of the resurrection of his body to eternal life." (p. 11.)
- "There will be an awakening of the body and a resurrection of a spiritual body capable of and fitted
  for eternal life." (p. 39.)
- "The doctrine of eternal life permeates all the mys-
  teries of Freemasonry; it is the fundamental basis of
  the Third Degree in a very special emphasis. Co-equal
  with emphasis on this tenet of Masonic faith is belief
  in the future resurrection of the body." (p. 41.)
- "A distinctive tenet of Masonry is that there remains
  a heaven of rest and of rewards for the good and
  faithful, a place of perfect happiness beyond the grave
  and the resurrection of the body." (p. 44.)
- "The very philosophy of Masonry teaches us that
  there can be no death without a resurrection, no
  decay without a subsequent restoration, no loss without eventual recovery." (p. 49.)
- "This collection of metaphors is a part of the scripture reading of the Third Degree and forms an appropriate introduction to the sublime ceremonies whose
  object is to teach symbolically the resurrection and
  life eternal." (p. 58.)

Freemasonry's Doctrine of Bodily Resurrection Is Heretical

Both the uniqueness of Jesus Christ and the Catholic doctrine of the Resurrection of the Body are divine truths taught by the Catholic Church, and they must be equally believed. Both truths "come from the same Author and Master."[11] Freemasonry holds to one (resurrection), *but not to the other (Jesus Christ)*. As Pope Pius XI states, "Are these truths not equally certain, or not equally to be believed . . . ? Has not God revealed them all?"[12]

Catholics cannot accept "revelations" or legends that claim to surpass or correct the revelation of Christ.[13] Because Freemasonry deliberately omits Christ from its dogma of bodily resurrection, its teachings on resurrection are heretical, that is, false because contrary to truths of divine revelation taught by the Catholic Church. Catholics objectively commit the sin of heresy by swearing oaths to adhere to heretical teachings.[14] By committing heresy, a Catholic commits a mortal sin and loses the life of Sanctifying Grace, placing himself under God's condemnation. Thus, Pope Leo XIII warns Catholics to renounce Freemasonry "or remain separated from Christian communion and lose their soul now and for eternity."[15]

—13—
The Clear, Consistent Teaching of the Church

The Church's Teachings Are Infallible

As we have seen, 12 Popes have condemned Freemasonry over the last 250 years on the grounds that Masonry's teachings are incompatible with Catholic faith and morals. As Bl. Pius IX declared, the Church's "decrees refer not only to Masonic groups in Europe, *but also those in America* and in other regions of the world."[1] The Church's repeated condemnations of the errors of Indifferentism, Naturalism and Modernism, which are inculcated through Masonic teaching, are part of the Church's infallible Ordinary Magisterium and thus are binding on all Catholics. Catholics must adhere to these teachings in order to remain Catholics and in order to maintain communion with the Catholic Church.

For example: Freemasonry rejects the Catholic Church's teachings that there is only one God, the Blessed Trinity; that Jesus Christ is the one way of salvation; and that there is "No salvation outside the Church" (understood in the way the Church has always understood this teaching). However, Catholics must believe these truths—and many others—with Divine and Catholic faith. As Cardinal Ratzinger stated, the assent which a Catholic must give to the truths of Catholic doctrine is definitive and irrevocable.[2] To consider these teachings a matter of indifference is to reject the Catholic Faith altogether. If a Catholic rejects the Faith, he is no longer a Catholic, he is no longer in communion with the Church, and he is headed for eternal damnation unless he repents of his sin. Pope Gregory XVI declared:

> With the admonition of the apostle that "there is one Lord, one faith, one baptism," may those fear who contrive the notion that the safe harbor of salvation is open to persons of any religion whatever. They should consider the testimony of Christ Himself that "those who are not with Christ are against Him," and that they disperse unhappily who do not gather with Him. Therefore, "without a doubt, *they will perish forever, unless they hold the Catholic Faith whole and inviolate.*"[3]

"Catholic" Masons and The Church's Canon Law

Although Freemasonry is one of the errors that has been most frequently condemned by the Church, some Catholics have become confused by changes in the Church's *Code of Canon Law.* Under the old 1917 Code (Canon 2335), any Catholic who enrolled in a Masonic sect or similar organization that plotted against the Church was automatically excommunicated.[4] The corresponding canon of the current, 1983 Code, Canon 1374, does not mention Masonry specifically and has changed the sanction from excommunication to a "just penalty" or an "interdict."[5] Because of these changes, some Catholics erroneously concluded that the Church had changed her position on Freemasonry. Nothing could be further from the truth.

Canon 1374 reads: "A person who joins an association which plots against the Church is to be punished with a just penalty; however, a person who promotes or directs an association of this kind is to be punished with an interdict."

The reason why the Church did not mention Masonry explicitly in Canon 1374 was to *broaden* the application of the law to cover *any* associations which plot against the Church. The arm of this law now reaches not only members of Freemasonry, but also members of any other organization that plots against the Church. The penalty for joining such organizations was changed from excommunication to "a just penalty" or "an interdict"—and, under this Canon, it is no longer incurred "automatically" but must be imposed by Church authority. However, "Catholic" Masons could still be automatically excommunicated under *other* provisions of the Code.[6]

For example, apostates, heretics and schismatics incur an excommunication *latae sententiae*—"automatically"—under Canon 1364.[7] The acts of apostasy, heresy or schism must be externally manifested and perceived (not only committed in the sinner's mind and will) in order to result in automatic excommunication. (See Canon 1330.) If a "Catholic" Mason knowingly and obstinately embraced the theology of the Lodge (Indifferentism, Naturalism), he would be guilty of heresy and automatically excommunicated. Similarly, if a Catholic knowingly and obstinately refused to acknowledge the Pope's authority to prohibit Masonic membership for Catholics (this is more than simply disobedience), he would automatically excommunicate himself from the Church as a schismatic. Catholics are subject to these penalties only if they obstinately persist in their sin. This means that the Catholic is aware of the Church's teaching (in the case of heresy) or of the authority of the Pope (in the case of schism) but persistently refuses to submit to it. Unfortunately, this is the case with many "Catholic" Masons today. If the Catholic did not act with full knowledge and consent, the penalty of excommunication or interdict would be mitigated or eliminated.[8]

The Church's 1983 "Declaration on Masonic Associations"

Because of the potential erroneous interpretations of the 1983 Code regarding Catholic membership in Freemasonry, the Congregation for the Doctrine of the Faith issued a "Declaration on Masonic Associations" on the day before the Code became effective. The document, which was written by Cardinal Joseph Ratzinger (the future Pope Benedict XVI) and approved by Pope John Paul II, reaffirms that Masonic principles are irreconcilable with the doctrine of the Church and that Catholic membership in Masonry remains forbidden. Following is the complete text of the declaration:

It has been asked whether there has been any change in the Church's decision in regard to Masonic associations since the new Code of Canon Law does not mention them expressly, unlike the previous Code.

This Sacred Congregation is in a position

to reply that this circumstance is due to an editorial criterion which was followed also in the case of other associations likewise unmentioned, inasmuch as they are contained in wider categories.

Therefore, the Church's negative judgment in regard to Masonic associations remains unchanged since their principles have always been considered irreconcilable with the doctrine of the Church and therefore membership in them remains forbidden. The faithful who enroll in Masonic associations are in a state of grave sin and may not receive Holy Communion. It is not within the competence of local ecclesiastical authorities to give a judgment on the nature of Masonic associations which would imply a derogation from what has been decided above, and this in line with the Declaration of this Sacred Congregation issued on 17 February 1981 (cf. AAS 73 (1981), pp. 240-241).

In an audience granted to Cardinal Ratzinger, the Supreme Pontiff John Paul II approved and ordered the publication of this Declaration which had been decided in an ordinary meeting of the Sacred Congregation.

Rome, from the Office of the Sacred Congregation for the Doctrine of the Faith, November 26, 1983.

On March 1, 2007, Bishop Gianfranco Girotti, the regent of the Apostolic Penitentiary, presided over a conference on the topic of Freemasonry at the St. Bonaventure Pontifical Theological Faculty. At the conference, Bishop Girotti reiterated the Church's 1983 condemnation of Freemasonry, stating that the concepts and philosophy of Masonry are incompatible with the Catholic Faith. For the Zenit News Agency article on the bishop's remarks, please see Appendix C.

"Catholic" Masons Who Receive the Eucharist Commit a Mortal Sin of Sacrilege

Not only does the 1983 Declaration restate the Church's constant opposition to Freemasonry, it also makes clear that Catholics who join the Masonic Lodge are in a state of grave sin (mortal sin) and may not receive Holy Communion.[9] Because it is the duty of all grave sinners to avoid the sacrilegious reception of Christ's Body and Blood, "Catholic" Masons cannot partake of the Eucharist. Moreover, pastors can and should refuse Holy Communion to those "Catholic" Masons who obstinately persist in their Masonic membership.[10] Those Catholics who are aware of their sin must receive absolution in Confession—the Sacrament of Penance— before being able to receive Holy Communion again.[11] In order for his Confession to be valid, the "Catholic" Mason must renounce his Masonic membership.

Being precluded from receiving the Eucharist is an extremely grave consequence of Catholic membership in Freemasonry. By choosing the Masonic Lodge over the Eucharist, "Catholic" Masons rupture their personal relationship with Jesus Christ and expel Sanctifying Grace from their souls. The Council of Trent infallibly declared that the Sacraments are not superfluous but are "necessary for salvation."[12] This teaching affirms Jesus Christ's teaching: "Amen, amen I say unto you, except you eat the flesh of the Son of man and drink his blood, you shall not have life in you."

(*John* 6:54). The Mason who continues to receive the Eucharist in a state of mortal sin "eats and drinks judgment to himself." (*1 Corinthians* 11:29). St. Paul's use of the word "judgment" (Greek, *krima*) refers to nothing less than *eternal condemnation.*[13]

Catholics Are Prohibited from Associating with Freemasons

Catholics must avoid not only joining the Masonic Lodge, but associating with Masons in any way. In his condemnation of Freemasonry, which he declared "valid forever," Pope Clement XII strictly commanded Catholics never to "be present" among Masons but to "stay completely clear" of any kind of association with them.[14] Pope Leo XIII also warned that "everyone should avoid familiarity or friendship with anyone suspected of belonging to Masonry or to affiliated groups."[15] (These groups include the Order of the Eastern Star for women, DeMolay for boys, Job's Daughters for girls, and any other group that is associated with Masonry or espouses Masonic ideology.) Pope Pius XI further reminds us that the Apostle John, who ceaselessly taught us to "love one another," forbade any intercourse with those who professed a corrupt version of Christ's teaching. (*2 John* 1:9-11).[16]

Some Catholic groups such as the Knights of Columbus hold joint gatherings with Shriners and other Masons.[17] Masons deliberately seek out these gatherings with Catholics in order to convince the public of Freemasonry's legitimacy. As we said in the beginning of this book, most people's knowledge of Masonry comes only from Masons and from the perceptions which Masons perpetuate. If people see joint assemblies of Catholics and Masons, they may believe that the

Church permits such association and even Catholic membership in the Lodge. Such gatherings are scandalous to the Faithful and prohibited by the Church. Catholics who associate with Masons must "know and understand that the shameful yoke of Freemasonry must be shaken off once and for all."[18]

—14—

Conclusion

"You can no longer ignore such incompatibility between Catholic and Mason, beloved children: You have been warned openly by Our predecessors, and We have loudly repeated the warning." —Pope Leo XIII[1]

The purpose of this book has been to present the teaching of the Catholic Church with regard to Catholicism and Freemasonry. It is hoped that this work "tore from the face of Masonry the mask which it used to hide itself and . . . showed it in its crude deformity and dark fatal activity."[2] We have seen that Freemasonry promotes the insidious doctrine of Indifferentism, according to which false religions are viewed as equally serviceable alternatives to the True Religion of Jesus Christ. If that were not enough, Masonry has created its own doctrines about God, man and resurrection which are incompatible with the Catholic Faith. These doctrines should be offensive to the faith and reason of any professing Catholic.

Like all of her condemnations of error, the Church's opposition to Freemasonry is born out of her love and zeal for souls. As a loving Mother, the Church seeks to protect her children from the deceits of the enemy. Whereas many Masons claim that Freemasonry is

58

merely a "fraternity," the fact remains that religious error is error, *no matter what the context.* Errors on matters of salvation lead souls to eternal perdition. Catholics involved in Freemasonry must heed the Church's warning: "Let no man think that he may for any reason whatsoever join the Masonic sect, if he values his Catholic name and his eternal salvation as he ought to value them."[3]

Many good men have been deceived by the allurements and vices of Freemasonry. As they become more involved in the Lodge, they tend to grow apathetic and lukewarm in their Catholic faith.[4] The more knowledge we Catholics have about Freemasonry, the more effective we can be in bearing witness to the Truth. The stakes cannot be any higher than eternal salvation. Let us pray, therefore, for the courage and conviction to confront the errors of Masonry whenever and wherever we meet them. Let us also pray for the grace of conversion for all those who have been deceived by Masonry's malevolent designs.

May the Triumph of the Immaculate Heart of Mary crush the heresy of Freemasonry now and forever!

Further Reading

For more information about Freemasonry and the Catholic Faith, as well as about my journey out of the Lodge, I recommend my book *Masonry Unmasked: An Insider Reveals the Secrets of the Lodge* (Our Sunday Visitor, 2006, 222 pages). To order, call Our Sunday Visitor at 1.800.348.2440 or visit their website at www.osv.com.

Appendix A

Papal Condemnations of Freemasonry

- Pope Clement XII, *In Eminenti* (1738).
- Pope Benedict XIV, *Providas* (1751).
- Pope Pius VI, *Inscrutabile* (1775).
- Pope Pius VII, *Ecclesiam Christi* (1821).
- Pope Leo XII, *Quo Graviora* (1826).
- Pope Pius VIII, *Traditi Humilitati* (1829).
- Pope Gregory XVI, *Mirari Vos* (1832).
- Bl. Pope Pius IX, *Qui Pluribus* (1846).
- Bl. Pope Pius IX, *Inter Multiplices* (1853).
- Bl. Pope Pius IX, *Quanto Conficiamur Moerore* (1863).
- Bl. Pope Pius IX, *Quanta Cura* (1864).
- Bl. Pope Pius IX, *Etsi Multa* (1873).
- Pope Leo XIII, *Etsi Nos* (1882).
- Pope Leo XIII, *Humanum Genus* (1884). This famous encyclical gives a thorough exposition of the Catholic teaching on Freemasonry.
- Pope Leo XIII, *Officio Sanctissimo* (1887).
- Pope Leo XIII, *Dell'alto dell'Apostolico Seggio* (1890).
- Pope Leo XIII, *Custodi di Quella Fede* (1892).
- Pope Leo XIII, *Inimica Vis* (1892).
- Pope Leo XIII, *Praeclara Gratulationis Publicae* (1894).
- Pope St. Pius X, *Vehementer Nos* (1906).

- Pope St. Pius X, *Une Fois Encore* (1907).
- Pope Pius XI, *Maximam Gravissimamque* (1924).
- Congregation for the Doctrine of the Faith under Pope John Paul II, *Quaesitum Est* (1983).

Appendix B

"No Salvation Outside The Church"

Papal and Conciliar Documents that Deal with the Catholic Doctrine of "No Salvation Outside the Church" (In Latin, *Extra ecclesiam nulla salus [est]*).

- Athanasian Creed (c.400).
- Pope Pelagius, *Quod ad dilectionem ad episcopos schismaticos* (c.585).
- Pope St. Gregory the Great, *Moralia in Iob,* XIV:5 (c.590).
- Pope Innocent III, *Apostolicae Sedis Primatus ad Iohannem* (1199).
- Fourth Lateran Council under Pope Innocent III (1215).
- Pope Boniface VIII, *Unam Sanctam* (1302).
- Pope Eugene IV, *Cantate Domino* (1441).
- Pope Leo XII, *Ubi Primum* (1825).
- Pope Pius VIII, *Traditi Humilitati Nostrae* (1829).
- Pope Gregory XVI, *Summo Iugiter Studio* (1832).
- Bl. Pope Pius IX, *Singulari Quadam* (1854).
- Bl. Pope Pius IX, *Quanto Conficiamur Moerore* (1863).
- Bl. Pope Pius IX, *Syllabus of Errors* (1864).

- Pope Leo XIII, *Annum Ingressi Sumus* (1902).
- Pope St. Pius X, *Jucunda Sane* (1904).
- Pope St. Pius X, *Catechism of Pope St. Pius X* (1903-1914).
- Pope Benedict XV, *Ad Beatissimi Apostolorum* (1914).
- Pope Pius XI, *Mortalium Animos* (1928).
- Pope Pius XII, *Allocution to the Gregorian* (1953).
- Second Vatican Council under Pope Paul VI, *Lumen Gentium* (1964).

Appendix C

Recent Restatement of the Church's Condemnation

Regent Restates Vatican's Anti-Masonry Position: Says Its Philosophies Are Incompatible with the Church

ROME, MARCH 2, 2007 (Zenit.org). The Church has not changed its ruling on Catholic membership in the Masons, said the regent of the Apostolic Penitentiary.

Bishop Gianfranco Girotti made this statement Thursday at a conference on the topic of Freemasonry held at the St. Bonaventure Pontifical Theological Faculty.

The bishop presided over the congress held in co-operation with the Socio-Religious Research and Information Group of Italy. Officials of Masonic associations and grand masters also took part in the meeting.

Bishop Girotti reminded his listeners that the Church has always criticized the concepts and philosophy of Freemasonry, considering them incompatible with the Catholic faith.

He mentioned the last official reference document, "Declaration on Masonic Associations," which was signed by the then prefect of the Congregation for the Doctrine of the Faith, Cardinal Joseph Ratzinger, on Nov. 26, 1983.

The text states that since the principles of Masonic associations "have always been considered irreconcilable with the doctrine of the Church," membership in them, therefore, "remains forbidden."

"The faithful who enroll in Masonic associations are in a state of grave sin and may not receive holy Communion," adds the declaration signed by Cardinal Ratzinger, who is now Benedict XVI.

Father Zbigniew Suchecki, an expert in the subject, quoted number 1374 of the Code of Canon Law, which reads: "Whoever is inscribed in an association that plots against the Church must be punished with a just penalty; whoever promotes or directs that association, must be banned [also translated as: "punished with an interdict"]."

"Masonry's attempts to express divine truths are based on relativism and do not agree with the principles of the Christian faith," said the Conventual Franciscan.

Bishop Girotti made reference to the statements of some priests who have declared publicly their membership in Masonry and called for the intervention of "their direct superiors," not excluding the possibility that "measures of a canonical character might come from the Holy See."

Appendix D

Resigning from Freemasonry

The first step a Catholic must take to sever his affiliation with Freemasonry is to renounce his Masonic membership by confessing it in the Sacrament of Penance (Sacrament of Reconciliation). Jesus Christ instituted the Sacrament of Penance when He declared to His Apostles, "Whose sins you shall forgive, they are forgiven them; and whose sins you shall retain, they are retained." (*John* 20:23). The Church teaches that a person must confess in this Sacrament "all the unconfessed grave sins [that is, mortal sins] he has committed."[1] Because Catholic membership in Masonry is a "grave sin" (see p. 54 above), the Catholic must be absolved of this sin in Confession.

The Catholic must also confess the sins which he committed by swearing Masonic oaths. The Masonic oaths are sinful because they invoke God's Holy Name in trivial matters and, worse, call Him to approve the grave sin of making a commitment to Freemasonry.[2] (See pp. 35-36 above.) The Masonic self-curses, sworn on the Holy Scriptures, exacerbate the gravity of the sin. Masonry considers the Mason bound in a "Masonic covenant" after he takes a Masonic oath.[3] The self-curses could potentially carry with them attendant spiritual evils from which deliverance is necessary. However, normally the absolution received in the Sacrament of Penance frees a Catholic from any evil spiritual connection with Freemasonry. Incidentally, as mentioned earlier, an oath to do something sinful is not morally binding. "No obligation arises from an oath to do something that is forbidden or useless."[4] It is a grave sin to take an oath to do something gravely sinful, and it is a sin to carry out a sinful oath.

The second step the Catholic should take is to write a letter of resignation to the lodge in which he was initiated. Because the degrees conferred in the Blue Lodge are prerequisites to receiving advanced degrees (such as those conferred by the Scottish or York Rite), resigning from the Blue Lodge automatically terminates a man's membership in any other Masonic organizations. In most states, Masonic law requires the Secretary of the lodge to read the letter of resignation aloud to all who are present at the meeting. This provides a unique opportunity to educate the membership about the incompatibility of Freemasonry with Christianity. Such a letter may also move the hearts of men who are searching for the truth.

There is no template or form letter that must be used. In fact, a resignation letter is not required by the Church, only recommended. Also, those who choose to write a letter do not have to state their reasons for resigning. Nevertheless, the chance to confess one's love for Jesus Christ and to help win souls for God through a letter that will be read in the lodge should not be overlooked. Our Blessed Lord said, "Everyone therefore that shall confess me before men, I will also confess him before my Father who is in heaven. But he that shall deny me before men, I will also deny him before my Father who is in heaven." (*Matthew* 10:32; see also *Luke* 12:8-9).

Following is a sample letter of resignation:

To the Members of _____ Lodge No. _____:

This letter is to inform you of my resignation from Freemasonry. I can no longer be a Mason because the teachings of Masonry are incompatible with the Christian Faith. Freemasonry teaches that a Mason can merit eternal life with God no matter what religion he professes. This is contrary to the religion of Jesus Christ, who declared, "I am the way, and the truth, and the life. No man cometh to the Father, but by me." (*John* 14:6).

Freemasonry's religious errors are numerous and profound. For example, Freemasonry teaches that God is the Grand Architect of the Universe who is worshiped in all religions. The Catholic Church teaches that God is Father, Son and Holy Ghost; that Jesus Christ is God the Son Incarnate; and that God must be worshiped within the Catholic Church, which He founded. Freemasonry teaches that all men are on an equal footing in their prayers to God, in spite of their religious errors and sinful lifestyles. In the Catholic Church, prayer is a covenant relationship between God and man in Christ which begins at Baptism and is maintained only through a life lived in the state of Sanctifying Grace.

Freemasonry teaches that the Bible is a mere symbol of God's will and can be replaced by other religious books which express that same will. The Church teaches that the Bible is the inspired and inerrant Word of God and that the books of other religions are man-made and contain grave errors. Freemasonry teaches that a man's own purity of life and conduct allows him to enter the "celestial lodge above." The Church teaches that a man must be baptized into Jesus Christ and must die in the state of Sanctifying Grace in order to save his soul. Freemasonry teaches that a good Mason will be resurrected to heaven without any need to believe in or obey Jesus Christ. The Church teaches that a man who does not respond to God's grace in Jesus Christ can have no hope of eternal life.

While Freemasonry claims to promote and foster charity, nothing can be *less* charitable than teaching errors which can lead a soul to eternal damnation. Freemasonry's doctrine that a man can gain eternal life without Jesus Christ is such an error—in fact, *the most grievous of all errors.* Jesus Christ said, "No man can serve two masters. For either he will hate the one, and love the other: or he will sustain the one, and despise the other. You cannot serve God and mammon." (*Matthew* 6:24; see also *Luke* 16:13).

A Christian cannot serve the God of truth and the mammon of Freemasonry. He must choose one or the other. I have chosen Jesus Christ, and that choice is what I wish for all of you.

In Christ Jesus,

Former Mason _____

(Name)

Notes

1. A Harmless Fraternal Organization? (p. 1)

1. Pope Leo XIII, *Custodi di Quella Fede* (1892), No. 10.
2. Wisconsin Multiple Letter Cipher, 56.
3. Pope Pius IX, *Etsi Multa* (1873), No. 30.
4. Pope Leo XII, *Quo Graviora* (1826), No 6.
5. All Scripture quotations are taken from the Douay-Rheims version of the Bible.
6. Pope Boniface VIII, *Unam Sanctam* (1302).
7. Pope Leo XIII, *Humanum Genus* (1884), No. 31.

2. The History and Purpose of Freemasonry (p. 5)

1. *Heirloom Masonic Bible,* Master Reference Edition. (Wichita, KS: DeVore & Sons, Inc., 1988), p. 56 (hereafter the *Masonic Bible*).
2. Ibid., p. 26.
3. Albert G. Mackey, *Mackey's Revised Encyclopedia of Freemasonry*, Revised and Enlarged by Robert I. Clegg, Vol. 1 (Richmond, VA: Macoy, 1966), p. 499.
4. Henry Wilson Coil, *Coil's Masonic Encyclopedia* (New York: Macoy, 1961), p. 512. The works of, *inter alia*, Mackey, Coil, and Albert Pike are also the authorities the Catholic Church has used in its studies on Freemasonry. See, for example, William J. Whalen, "The Pastoral Problem of Masonic Membership," *Origens*, 15/6 (June 27, 1985), pp. 84-92.
5. The related acronym is A.A.O.N.M.S. These letters are placed on large signs and rearranged in Shrine ritual to spell A. M.A.S.O.N. In this way, the Shriners emphasize that their organization is Masonic.
6. While Shriners often boast about their sponsorship of hospitals for sick children, the Shrine's charitable activities have been criticized. For example, the *Orlando Sentinel* reported that the Shrine generated $23 million in 1985 from its circus parades but gave less than two percent to medical care for children (August 3,7; September 15, 1985). Ann Landers reported this same story in the article "Shrine Records Shocking" (*South Haven Daily Tribune*, April 24, 1987).

7. *Mackey's Revised Encyclopedia of Freemasonry*, Vol. 2, p. 859.

3. An Introduction to the Errors of Freemasonry (p. 9)

1. See Pope Pius IX, *Quanto Conficiamur Moerore* (1863), No. 7.
2. The Council of Trent, when setting forth the necessity of Baptism as proclaimed by Christ in *John* 3:5, states that Baptism *or its desire* is necessary. (Session 6, chap. 4.) Found in *Canons and Decrees of the Council of Trent* (St. Louis: B. Herder, 1941; reprint, TAN, 1978), p. 31.
3. Pope Pius IX, *Syllabus of Errors* (1864), No. 17. The Catholic Church cannot presume the good faith of those who deliberately remain outside her visible structure, due to their external dissidence. Nevertheless, God alone judges the interior realities of a person's conscience, whether or not he is invincibly ignorant, and whether he may somehow be "inside" the Catholic Church.
4. Wisconsin Multiple Letter Cipher, p. 85.
5. Ibid., pp. 88-89.
6. This usage is generally limited to English-speaking lodges.
7. *The Short Talk Bulletin*, "Behind the Symbol," Vol. 32, No. 7 (1954).
8. Wisconsin Multiple Letter Cipher, 91.
9. *The Short Talk Bulletin*, "The Letter G," Vol. 5, No. 7 (1927).
10. First Vatican Council, Session 3, Canon 2, *On Revelation* (1870).
11. *Masonic Bible*, p. 38.
12. Pope Pius IX, *Qui Pluribus* (1846), No. 5; *Quanta Cura* (1864), No. 3; Pope Leo XIII, *Humanum Genus* (1884), No. 12; *Officio Sanctissimo* (1887), No. 7; *Inimica Vis* (1892), No. 8; *Custodi di Quella Fede* (1892), No. 4; Pope Pius XI, *Mortalium Animos* (1928), No. 2.
13. Pope Leo XIII, *Humanum Genus* (1884), No. 12.
14. Ibid., *Custodi di Quella Fede* (1892), No. 4.
15. Albert Pike, *Morals and Dogma of the Ancient and Accepted Scottish Rite of Freemasonry* (Charleston, SC: Supreme Council of the Thirty-third Degree for the Southern Jurisdiction of the United States, 1881), pp. 104-105 (emphasis added). Pike also said that "Catholicism was a vital truth in its earliest ages, but it became obsolete." Ibid., p. 38.
16. Martin L. Wagner, *Freemasonry: An Interpretation* (Dahlonega, GA.: Crown Rights Book Company, 1912), p. 153 (emphasis added).
17. Pope Leo XIII, *Testem Benevolentiae Nostrae* (1899).
18. Pope Pius X, *Pascendi Dominici Gregis* (1907), No. 3 (emphasis added).
19. Ibid., No. 39.
20. Joseph Fort Newton, *The Builders: A Story and Study of Freemasonry* (Cedar Rapids, IA: The Torch Press, 1915; reprint Richmond, VA: Macoy, 1951), p. 243.

21. Albert G. Mackey, *An Encyclopedia of Freemasonry* (Philadelphia: L.H. Everts, 1887), p. 731.
22. Ibid.
23. *Louisiana Monitor* (1980), p. 133.
24. Pope Pius XI , *Mortalium Animos* (1928), No. 2.
25. Pope Gregory XVI, *Mirari Vos* (1832), No. 13. See also Pope Pius VII, *Ecclesiam Christi* (1821); Pope Pius VIII, *Traditi Humilitati* (1829), No. 4; and Pope Pius IX, *Qui Pluribus* (1846), Nos. 5-6.
26. Pope Pius IX, *Quanto Conficiamur Moerore* (1863), No. 7. See also Pope Pius IX, *Multiplices Inter* (1851) and *Maxima Quidem* (1862).
27. Pope Leo XIII, *Humanum Genus* (1884), No. 21.
28. Ibid., No. 16. See also Pope Pius IX, *Allocution to the Consistory* (1861).
29. Pope Pius XI, *Mortalium Animos* (1928), No. 2. See also the *Catechism of the Catholic Church* (CCC), Second Edition (Washington, DC: United States Catholic Converence, Inc., 1997), No. 2128.
30. See, for example, Pope Leo XIII, *Satis Cognitum* (1896); Pope Pius XII, *Mystici Corporis Christi* (1943); *Humani Generis* (1950).
31. Pope Pius IX, *Etsi Multa* (1873), No. 28.

4. Preparation for the First Degree (p. 18)

1. Wisconsin Multiple Letter Cipher, p. 47.

5. Spiritual Darkness (p. 20)

1. Wisconsin Multiple Letter Cipher, p. 35.
2. *Masonic Bible,* p. 39 (emphasis added).
3. Ibid., p. 49.
4. Allen E. Roberts, *The Craft and Its Symbols: Opening the Door to Masonic Symbolism* (Richmond, VA: Macoy, 1974), p. 13 (emphasis added).
5. Albert G. Mackey, *Masonic Ritualist* (New York: Clark & Maynard, 1869), p. 23 (emphasis added).
6. See also *John* 1:4,5,7-9; 3:19; 9:5; 12:35-36,46; *1 John* 1:5,7; 2:8-10.
7. *John* 3:5. See also *1 Corinthians* 6:11; *Titus* 3:5-7; *Hebrews* 10:22; *1 Peter* 3:21.
8. See St. Justin Martyr, *First Apology,* 61; St. Clement of Alexandria, *The Instructor of Children*; St. Gregory Nazianzen; CCC, No. 1216.
9. See also *Matthew* 5:14,16; 6:23; *Luke* 11:34; 16:8; *Acts* 26:18; *Romans* 13:12; *2 Corinthians* 4:6; *Ephesians* 5:8-9; *Colossians* 1:12.
10. See also CCC, Nos. 1216, 1265, 1267.

11. Wisconsin Multiple Letter Cipher, p. 36.

6. Freemasonry's Worship of "Deity" (p. 24)

1. Wisconsin Multiple Letter Cipher, p. 36.
2. See *John* 14:13-14; CCC, No. 2664.
3. *Short Talk Bulletin,* "The Holy Bible," Vol. 2 (1924), No. 3.
4. Manly P. Hall, *The Lost Keys of Freemasonry; or, The Secret of Hiram Abiff* (Richmond, VA: Macoy, 1976), p. 65.
5. See, for example, *John* 1:1-3,14,18; 8:58; 10:30; *Acts* 2:36; 3:15; 20:28; *Romans* 9:5; *Colossians* 2:9; *Titus* 2:13; 3:4; *Hebrews* 1:6,8-9; *2 Peter* 1:1; *1 John* 5:20; *Apocalypse* 2:8.
6. Pope Pius XI, *Mortalium Animos* (1928), No. 10. See also Pope Clement VIII, *Magnus Dominus* (1595); Pope Leo XIII, *Praeclara Gratulationis Publicae* (1894); *Testem Benevolentiae Nostrae* (1899); Pope Pius X, *Ex Quo* (1910); and Pope Pius XII, *Sommamente Gradita* (1942); *Mystici Corporis* (1943). In these documents, the Popes declare the necessity for Protestants and the Orthodox to return to the Roman Catholic Church to save their souls.
7. Second Vatican Council, *Unitatis Redintegratio* (1964), No. 8. Cf. Fr. Heribert Jone, O.F.M. Cap.: "The natural law forbids participation in services that are heretical. If the service is one that heretics have in common with us, even though no scandal comes from such participation, it is at least forbidden by Church law."—*Moral Theology* (Westminster, MD: Newman Press, 1962; TAN rpt., 1993), No. 125, p. 70.
8. CCC, No. 2564.
9. *Summa Theologica II-II,* Question 83 (Of Prayer), Article 16. St. Thomas says that God may, out of mercy, hear the prayer of a sinner for something "pertaining to godliness." In particular, St. Thomas says that God hears the prayer of a sinner if he "beseech for himself things necessary for salvation, piously and perseveringly." (Ibid). See *John* 9:31; *Psalms* 66:18; *Proverbs* 15:29; 28:9; *Isaias* 1:15.
10. Pope John Paul II, *Redemptoris Missio* (1990), No. 5.
11. Cf. CCC, No. 1124.
12. See Congregation for the Doctrine of the Faith, *Dominus Iesus* (2000), No. 21.

7. Who Is the God of Freemasonry? (p. 28)

1. *Masonic Bible,* p. 42.
2. Wisconsin Multiple Letter Cipher, p. 93.
3. *The Lost Keys of Freemasonry; or, The Secret of Hiram Abiff,* p. 65.
4. *Coil's Masonic Encyclopedia,* p. 27.
5. *Short Talk Bulletin,* "All-Seeing Eye," Vol. 10, No. 12 (1932).
6. *Masonic Bible,* p. 63.

7. *Coil's Masonic Encyclopedia*, p. 516.
8. Oliver Street, "Freemasonry in Foreign Lands," *Little Masonic Library* (Kingsport, TN: Southern Publishers, Inc., 1946), Vol. 1, p. 135.

8. Freemasonry's Profession of Faith in the Deity (p. 31)

1. Wisconsin Multiple Letter Cipher, p. 37.
2. Ibid.
3. Carl Claudy, "Entered Apprentice," *Introduction to Freemasonry*, Vol. 1, p. 38.
4. *Masonic Bible*, p. 44.
5. *The Short Talk Bulletin*, "Masonic Geometry," Vol. 12, No. 5, 1934.
6. Pope Pius IX, *Qui Pluribus* (1846), No 6.
7. Pope Pius VIII, *Traditi Humilitati* (1829), No. 4.

9. Freemasonry's Oaths (p. 34)

1. *Masonic Bible*, p. 32.
2. Nevada Ritual, p. 19 (Entered Apprentice oath).
3. Wisconsin Multiple Letter Cipher, p. 79 (Fellowcraft oath).
4. Ibid., p. 114 (Master Mason oath).
5. The candidate for the Shriners swears this self-curse to the god Allah on the Koran. Note also that Shriners meet in Mosques, wear Islamic vestments, use Islamic symbols like the crescent and scimitar, and use the secret passwords *Mecca* and *Medina*. In light of these practices, either the Shriners mock the religion of Islam or they sincerely incorporate elements of Islamic religious practice.
6. CCC, Nos. 2150, 2155; see also Nos. 1756, 1856.
7. No. 186, par. 2 (p. 117). The terms "mortal sin" and "grave sin" mean the same thing.
8. Ibid., No. 187, par. I (p. 117).
9. See CCC, No. 2155; see also No. 2149; *Matthew* 5:34-37; *James* 5:12. Fr. Jone states that there must be a *sufficient reason* to take an oath. (*Moral Theology*, No. 186, par. 3, p. 117).
10. Wisconsin Multiple Letter Cipher, p. 113 (Master Mason oath).
11. Ibid.
12. See CCC, Nos. 2148, 2149.
13. Pope Benedict XIV, *Providas* (1751).
14. Pope Leo XII, *Quo Graviora* (1826).
15. *Masonic Bible*, p. 24.

10. Freemasonry's View of the Holy Bible (p. 38)

1. Wisconsin Multiple Letter Cipher, p. 41.
2. Ibid.
3. *Coil's Masonic Encyclopedia*, p. 520.

4. George Chase Wingate, *Digest of Masonic Law*, Third Edition (New York: Macoy and Sickles, 1864), p. 206 (emphasis added).
5. *Short Talk Bulletin*, "The Holy Bible," Vol. 2, March, 1924, No. 3.
6. *An Encyclopedia of Freemasonry*, p. 114.
7. CCC, No. 105 (emphasis in original); see also *2 Timothy* 3:16.
8. The Council of Trent, *Decree Concerning the Canonical Scriptures* (1546), Session 4; First Vatican Council, *On Revelation* (1870), Session 3, Chapter 2.
9. Pope Leo XIII, *Providentissimus Deus* (1893), No. 20.

11. Freemasonry's Salvation by Works (p. 41)

1. *Minnesota Masonic Manual*, p. 20 (emphasis added).
2. *Wisconsin Multiple Letter Cipher*, p. 53.
3. Ibid., p. 46.
4. Pope Gregory XVI, *Mirari Vos* (1832), No. 13 (emphasis added).
5. See *Romans* 5:12,19.
6. Council of Trent, Session 6, Canon 1, *Decrees on Justification* (1547). (Included in *Canons and Decrees of the Council of Trent*, p. 42).
7. See *1 Corinthians* 15:45.
8. See *Romans* 5:1-2; *Titus* 3:5-7.
9. See CCC, No. 679.
10. See CCC, No. 1992.
11. See CCC, No. 1996.
12. See CCC, Nos. 2007-2010. In fact, no one can merit the initial *actual grace* (the initial actual grace is sometimes called "prevenient grace") which is at the origin of conversion. (CCC, No. 2027). However, after a person responds to the initial grace which leads him to repentance and Baptism, he receives Sanctifying Grace. In the state of Sanctifying Grace, he can merit further grace and can merit eternal life; but even this supernatural *meriting* is a gift from God. See Council of Trent, Session 6, Canons 3, 32. (*Canons and Decrees of the Council of Trent*, pp. 42, 46).

12. Freemasonry's Doctrine of Resurrection of the Body (p. 45)

1. *Masonic Bible*, p. 49.
2. Ibid., p. 55 (emphasis added).
3. While the Hiramic Legend is a mere legend and not actual history, the historical character named Hiram Abif is mentioned in Scripture in *1 Kings* 7:13-14 and *2 Paralipomenon* (*2 Chronicles*) 2:14; 4:16.
4. *Nevada Ritual*, p. 137.
5. *Masonic Bible*, p. 55 (emphasis added). See also *Mackey's Revised Encyclopedia of Freemasonry*, Vol. 2, p. 828, which describes the "raising" the same way.

6. Wisconsin Multiple Letter Cipher, p. 136 (emphasis added).
7. Ibid., p. 145 (emphasis added).
8. See *Matthew* 16:24; *Mark* 8:34; *Luke* 9:23.
9. CCC, No. 997; *Masonic Bible,* p. 11.
10. Pope Leo XIII, *Custodi di Quella Fede* (1892).
11. Pope Leo XIII, *Testem Benevolentiae Nostrae* (1899).
12. Pope Pius XI, *Mortalium Animos,* (1928), No. 9.
13. See CCC, No. 67.
14. See CCC, No. 2089. See also the entry for "Heresy" in the Glossary of this book.
15. Pope Leo XIII, *Custodi di Quella Fede* (1892), No. 11.

13. The Clear, Consistent Teaching of the Church (p. 50)

1. Pope Pius IX, *Etsi Multa* (1873), No. 30 (emphasis added).
2. Joseph Cardinal Ratzinger, Doctrinal Commentary issued June 29, 1998, coincident with *Ad tuendam fidem* of Pope John Paul II.
3. Pope Gregory XVI, *Mirari Vos* (1832), emphasis added. See also Pope Leo XIII, *Satis Cognitum* (1896) and Pope Pius X, *Ex Quo* (1910). In these documents also, the Popes declare that Catholics must hold to the *entire* Catholic Faith in order to remain Catholic and that whoever refuses even one of the truths of the Faith loses the entire Faith.
4. Can. 2335 (1917 code): "Those who have themselves enrolled in a Masonic sect or other associations of the same kind which plot against the Church or the legitimate civil powers incur *ipso facto* excommunication reserved simply to the Apostolic See."
5. Can. 1374 (1983 code; unless otherwise indicated, all citations herein of the Code of Canon Law (CIC) refer to the current (1983) code): "One who joins an association which plots against the Church is to be punished with a just penalty; one who promotes or moderates such an association is to be punished with an interdict." Canon Law Society of America, *New Commentary on the Code of Canon Law* (Mahwah, NJ: Paulist Press, 2000), p. 1583.
6. Note also that an interdict may have the same deleterious effects as an excommunication (i.e., those under interdict are forbidden to receive certain Sacraments).
7. CCC, No. 2089 and CIC, Can. 751 define apostasy as "the total repudiation of the Christian faith." Most "Catholic" Masons would not fulfill this definition.
8. Can. 1321, §1. For example, if a Catholic were invincibly ignorant of the Church's opposition to Freemasonry, he would not be subject to a penalty (Canon 1323, °2). Given the plethora of magisterial pronouncements condemning Freemasonry, invin-

cible ignorance should be a rare exception to the applicability of the penalties.

9. The Church has affirmed that those who die in a state of mortal sin are "tortured forever by the flames of eternal hell." Council of Lyons I (Dz. 457); see also Council of Florence (Dz. 693; 714); Pope Vigilius, *Canons Against Origen*, Can. 9 (Dz. 211).

10. See Canon 915, which says that Holy Communion is not to be given to those "obstinately persevering in manifest grave sin." See also *1 Corinthians* 11:27-30. Such Catholics are also forbidden to receive the Anointing of the Sick (Can. 1007), as well as ecclesiastical funeral rites if public scandal would result. (Can. 1184, §1, °3).

11. CCC, No. 1415.

12. "If anyone says that the sacraments of the New Law are not necessary for salvation but are superfluous, and that without them or without the desire of them men obtain from God through faith alone the grace of justification, though all are not necessary for each one, let him be anathema." Council of Trent, Session 7, Canon 4, Canons on the Sacraments in General (1547). (*Canons and Decrees of the Council of Trent*, p. 52.)

13. St. Paul also uses *krima* in *Romans* 5:16 to describe the eternal consequences of Adam's sin and in *1 Timothy* 3:6 when he warns bishops not to fall "into the judgment of the devil." See also *Matthew* 7:2; 23:14; *Mark* 12:40; *Luke* 20:47; 23:40; *John* 9:39; *Romans* 2:2-3; 3:8; *1 Timothy* 3:6; 5:12; *Hebrew* 6:2; *James* 3:1; *1 Peter* 4:17; *2 Peter* 2:3; *Judith* 4; *Apocalypse* 17:1; 18:20; 20:4.

14. Pope Clement XII, *In Eminenti* (1738). The *Masonic Bible* describes Pope Clement by stating that "a more bitter persecutor of masonry has not lived" (p. 26) and declares the Pope's condemnations to be "blasphemous and libelous to the utmost degree, preposterous and utterly false to the tenets and practices of the Order." (p. 13).

15. Pope Leo XIII, *Custodi di Quella Fede* (1892), No. 15.

16. Pope Pius XI, *Mortalium Animos* (1928), No. 9.

17. A common Mason/Knights assembly is called "All Faiths Night," properly recognizing that Freemasons are not of the same religious faith as the Knights of Columbus.

18. Pope Leo XIII, *Praeclara Gratulationis Publicae* (1894).

14. Conclusion (p. 58)

1. Pope Leo XIII, *Custodi di Quella Fede* (1892), No. 10.

2. Ibid., No. 2.

3. Pope Leo XIII, *Humanum Genus* (1884), No. 31.

4. If the "Catholic Mason" rejects the Church's teaching on Freemasonry and obstinately persists in his Masonic membership, God may blind him to the truth so that he cannot

understand it. See, for example, *Matthew* 11:25; 13:13-17; *Luke* 10:21-22; *John* 12:40; *Acts* 28:26-27; *Romans* 1:28; 11:8-10; *2 Thessalonians* 2:11-12; *Exodus* 10:1; *Isaias* 6:9-10; 44:18; *Jeremias* 6:21.

Appendix D: Resigning from Freemasonry (p. 66)

1. CCC, No. 1493.
2. See CCC, Nos. 2149, 2155.
3. *Masonic Bible,* p. 38.
4. *Moral Theology,* No. 187, par. I (p. 117).

Glossary of Terms

All-Seeing Eye—A Masonic symbol for the supreme deity.

Anathema—A Greek word which means to be set apart, excommunicated or accursed.

Apostasy—The total repudiation of the Christian Faith.

Apron—A garment worn around the waist for any formal Masonic assembly; it represents the purity of life and conduct necessary to gain admission into Heaven.

Ashlar—The Perfect Ashlar is a hewn, or squared, stone. It symbolizes the state of perfection at which a Mason arrives by his good works. The Rough Ashlar is a symbol of a Mason's rude and imperfect state by nature.

Blue Lodge—The body of Freemasonry that confers the degrees of Entered Apprentice, Fellowcraft, and Master Mason. It may also refer to a particular lodge under the jurisdiction of a Grand Lodge.

Cabletow—The rope a candidate wears during his initiation into the three degrees. In the Entered Apprentice Degree, the cabletow, worn around the candidate's neck, symbolizes his tie to the profane world. In the Fellowcraft and Master Mason Degrees, it is worn around the arm and waist, respectively, to symbolize the Mason's tie to the Lodge.

Celestial Lodge Above—Masonry's name for heaven.

Common Gavel—In Operative Masonry, the tool used to break off the corners of rough stones. In Speculative Masonry, a symbol of the Mason's effort to divest his mind and conscience of the vices and superfluities of life in order to become fit for heaven.

Degree—A particular level of Masonic status, conferred in a ceremony or ritual.

Divestiture—The rite in which a candidate for a Masonic degree removes his outer clothing worn in the profane world before being admitted into the Lodge.

Enlightenment—For Masons, the moment at which the hoodwink is removed from the Entered Apprentice after he has sworn the oath at the Masonic altar. For Christians, Enlightenment would mean receiving Baptism and the gift of faith, although Christians do not usually use the term "Enlightment." (The term "The Enlightenment" also refers to an 18th-century philosophic movement; the period of this movement was also known as "the Age of Reason.")

Entered Apprentice—One who has completed the First Degree of Blue Lodge Masonry.

Excommunication—A penalty or censure by which a baptized Roman Catholic is excluded from the communion of the faithful. According to Canon Law, an automatically excommunicated person is forbidden:

1. To have any ministerial participation in celebrating the sacrifice of the Eucharist or any other ceremonies of worship whatsoever;
2. To celebrate the sacraments or sacramentals and to receive the sacraments;
3. To exercise any ecclesiastical offices, ministries or functions whatsoever, or to place acts of governance. (Can. 1331).

Fellowcraft—One who has completed the Second Degree of Blue Lodge Masonry.

Five Senses—The rational means by which Masons know God (hearing, seeing, feeling, smelling and tasting).

Freemasonry—An esoteric religion of naturalism which teaches its principles through the symbolic use of operative stonemasons' tools.

The Letter G—The most common Masonic symbol for God in English-speaking countries. The letter *G* stands for God and Geometry.

GAOTU—An acronym for Masonry's name for God, the Grand (or Great) Architect of the Universe.

Geometry—In Freemasonry, the most revered of the sciences because it provides the surest proof of God's existence.

Grand Lodge—The supreme governing body of Freemasonry in a given jurisdiction. There are fifty-one Grand Lodges in the United States.

Great Lights—The Volume of the Sacred Law (usually the Holy Bible), the Square and Compass. The Great Lights are displayed during open lodge.

Heresy—a) The sin: The post-Baptismal wilful denial or wilful doubt of some truth which must be believed as a matter of Divine and Catholic faith. b) The eccleasiastical crime deserving of censure: The post-Baptismal, outwardly expressed, obstinate denial or obstinate doubt of some truth which must be believed as a matter of Divine and Catholic faith.

A truth of *Divine and Catholic faith* is a revealed truth presented by the Catholic Church for belief; examples are the truths in the Apostles' Creed.

Hiram Abif—In Masonic legend, the master-builder of King Solomon's Temple; the saviour, according to Freemasonry.

Hiramic Legend—The death-burial-and-resurrection rite of the Third Degree of Blue Lodge Masonry.

Hoodwink—The blindfold used during a candidate's initiation into Masonic degrees.

Indifferentism—A heresy which holds that one religion is as good as another and that all religions are equally legitimate paths to salvation.

Infallibility—A gift of the Holy Ghost whereby He prevents the Catholic Church from teaching error on matters of doctrine and morals, as promised by Jesus Christ.

Interdict—A penalty or censure by which a Catholic, while remaining in the communion of the faithful, is excluded from receiving or administering certain Sacraments and from holding certain sacred offices.

Jewels—Each lodge has six jewels, three immovable and three movable. The three immovable jewels are the Square, which teaches morality; the Level, which teaches equality; and the Plumb, which teaches rectitude of conduct. The three movable jewels are the Rough Ashlar, the Perfect Ashlar, and the Trestleboard.

Landmarks—The most fundamental and unalterable tenets of Freemasonry. These include a belief in deity (a god), immortality of the soul, resurrection of the body, oaths with self-curses, secrecy, and symbolism.

Master Mason—One who has completed the Third, and highest, degree of Blue Lodge Masonry.

Modernism—The synthesis of all heresies against the Catholic Faith. According to Modernism, the revealed truths of the Catholic Faith should be continually updated to conform to modern ideas and philosophies.

Naturalism—A heresy that views created Nature and human reason as the source of all the knowledge that man needs to know in order to reach Heaven and which denies the supernatural truths of the Catholic Faith.

Obligations—Masonic oaths sworn by the candidate as part of his initiation.

Officers of the Lodge—Worshipful Master, Senior and Junior Wardens, Senior and Junior Deacons, Senior and Junior Stewards, Tiler, Secretary, Treasurer (or Secretary-Treasurer), Lodge Counselor, and Chaplain. The Officers may also include a Marshal, Organist and Soloist.

Open Lodge—The time during which the lodge is "at labor" (i.e., performing rituals or conducting business), to be distinguished from the time when the lodge is "at refreshment" (i.e., closed or taking a break from its labors).

Operative Masonry—The building of physical structures by ancient stone masons.

Profane—One who has not been initiated into the degrees of Freemasonry, that is, a non-Mason.

Proficiency Man—One who has been formally recognized by his Grand Lodge as an expert in performing Masonic ritual and is authorized to give instruction in Masonic ritual.

Regular—That which is universally recognized by Freemasonry (for example, degrees, doctrines, symbols).

Schism—The refusal by a baptized Catholic to submit to the Pope or to be in communion with the members of the Church subject to the Pope.

Scottish Rite—An optional Masonic organization in which Master Masons can receive the 4th through the 32nd degree.

Sectarian—An accusation leveled at the Catholic Church by Freemasonry because the Church insists on particular doctrines, such as the universal and ultimate truth of the Revelation of Jesus Christ.

Setting Maul—In Masonic legend, the mallet used to murder Hiram Abif. The Setting Maul is a Masonic emblem of those casualties and diseases by which our earthly existence may be terminated.

Shriner—A 32nd Degree Scottish-Rite or York-Rite Mason. In their initiation ceremony, Shriners swear an oath to the god Allah on the Koran. Shriners are noted for their red fezzes, circus parades and sponsorship of hospitals.

Signs—The secret gestures that simulate the self-mutilation and death penalties carried by or connected to the Masonic oaths.

Speculative Masonry—The teaching of moral and religious truths, using operative stonemasons' tools and terminology, to build a man's spiritual temple, or soul.

Square—One of the Great Lights of Masonry. The tool used in Operative Masonry to square off the work. In Speculative Masonry, it symbolizes morality.

Symbolic Lodge—Blue Lodge.

Syncretism—A heresy which consolidates diverse and/or contradictory beliefs into a single system of belief.

Trestleboard—In Operative Masonry, the work plan of the Mason's architectural designs. In Speculative Masonry, the symbol of the Mason's spiritual and moral designs.

Volume of the Sacred Law—Any book placed on the Masonic altar that symbolizes God's will. In the United States, this book is typically the Holy Bible, but the Bible can be accompanied by or replaced by other religious writings.

Working Tools—The implements of Operative Masonry that are used to teach moral and spiritual truths to the Speculative Mason. These include the Common Gavel, Square, Level, Plumb and Trowel.

Worshipful Master—The highest officer of a Masonic lodge.

York Rite—An optional Masonic organization in which Master Masons can receive additional degrees conferred by the Royal Arch Chapter, the Council of Royal and Select Masters, and the Commandery of Knights Templar.

TAN · BOOKS

TAN Books was founded in 1967 to preserve the spiritual, intellectual and liturgical traditions of the Catholic Church. At a critical moment in history TAN kept alive the great classics of the Faith and drew many to the Church. In 2008 TAN was acquired by Saint Benedict Press. Today TAN continues its mission to a new generation of readers.

From its earliest days TAN has published a range of booklets that teach and defend the Faith. Through partnerships with organizations, apostolates, and mission-minded individuals, well over 10 million TAN booklets have been distributed.

More recently, TAN has expanded its publishing with the launch of Catholic calendars and daily planners—as well as Bibles, fiction, and multimedia products through its sister imprints Catholic Courses (CatholicCourses.com) and Saint Benedict Press (SaintBenedictPress.com).

Today TAN publishes over 500 titles in the areas of theology, prayer, devotions, doctrine, Church history, and the lives of the saints. TAN books are published in multiple languages and found throughout the world in schools, parishes, bookstores and homes.

For a free catalog, visit us online at
TANBooks.com

Or call us toll-free at
(800) 437-5876

Spread the Faith with . . .

TAN·BOOKS

A Division of Saint Benedict Press, LLC

TAN books are powerful tools for evangelization. They lift the mind to God and change lives. Millions of readers have found in TAN books and booklets an effective way to teach and defend the Faith, soften hearts, and grow in prayer and holiness of life.

Throughout history the faithful have distributed Catholic literature and sacramentals to save souls. St. Francis de Sales passed out his own pamphlets to win back those who had abandoned the Faith. Countless others have distributed the Miraculous Medal to prompt conversions and inspire deeper devotion to God. Our customers use TAN books in that same spirit.

If you have been helped by this or another TAN title, share it with others. Become a TAN Missionary and share our life changing books and booklets with your family, friends and community. We'll help by providing special discounts for books and booklets purchased in quantity for purposes of evangelization. Write or call us for additional details.

TAN Books
Attn: TAN Missionaries Department
PO Box 410487
Charlotte, NC 28241

Toll-free (800) 437-5876
missionaries@TANBooks.com